Presented to:

_____

From:

_____

Date:

_____

**Heavenly Promises
to "Me"**

✝ HEAVENLY PROMISES TO

"   "

―――――――――――――――――――――――――

«First Name» «Last Name»

Jeremiah 1:5 (KJV): ⁵ _____,
before I formed thee in the belly I knew thee;
and before thou camest forth out of the womb I
sanctified thee, _and_ I ordained thee...

1

Heavenly Promises
to "Me"

2

Heavenly Promises to me
Copyright 2008

Scripture quotations indentified KJV are from the Holy
Bible, King James Version®

Published by Lightning Source
1246 Heil Quaker Blvd.
LaVergne, TN 37086
www.lightningsource.com

Printed in the United States of America

ISBN- 978-0615-23246-1

 DEDICATION

We dedicate this promise book to our heavenly Father. We thank Him for the idea and the means to complete this awesome work and bring it to pass. This is the Lord's doing, and it is truly marvelous in our sight. Thank You, Father.

We would like to especially thank our spiritual parents in the Lord, Pastors Phillip and Cheryl Jackson of Grace Christian Center. Truly without them this book would not be possible. They have dedicated their lives to maturing God's children and teaching the body of Christ the move of the Holy Spirit. Most of what is expressed in this book is from their teachings and spiritual revelations. Because of them we now know and experience our blessed heavenly inheritance that has been given to us by the Father through faith in Christ Jesus, our Lord.

Pastors, with all of our hearts, THANK YOU!

Love, Dwain and Anita Byrum

3

 A NOTE TO THE READER

In an attempt to reveal the personal tone that the Father desires for us to experience through His Word, this book has been written in first person. We chose to write that which was pressed upon our hearts by the Father just as it was given to us—not as our thoughts and words, but His. God needs a man or woman to speak through, but all too often it is the voice of the person used that we hear, rather than the voice of God. By no means are we trying to pass off all that is written in this book as God's complete revelation, for we are mere vessels of clay doing our best to attain the mind of the God of this universe. Therefore, the promise Scriptures found in this book are not only used to build faith in your heart, but also to ensure that the content written in this book is confirmed by the Word of God.

As you read the text, please write your name in the spaces provided.

Your life will never be the same!

4

 TABLE OF CONTENTS

 INTRODUCTION

You, yes you, _____, I am calling you personally by name. Daily I am calling you into a deeper relationship and intimate fellowship with Me. You are important to Me. _____, I love you and desire to put My glory upon you and manifest Myself through you before the world, that it might see Me in you. I have saturated My Word with promises that are just for you, My child. On the pages of My Word, I have given you a glimpse into My character, position, and abilities. In it, I have exposed and expressed Myself in the lives of others to show what I can and will do for those who love, trust, and depend upon Me. However, all too often, My promises lie dormant on the pages of the Holy Bible and are passed off as just a good story or thought to be significant only for the person spoken of in the Bible. This is so far from the truth. My Word and My promises belong to you, _____. It is My Word that I look after to perform. It is My Word that will not return to Me void or unaccomplished. It is My Word that will not pass away. _____, My Word is POWERFUL! But this power is only activated in a believer, not a doubter. Believers take My Word personally. Believers remove the 2000-year-old setting and by faith pull it into the here and now. Believers understand that what Jesus did for them gives them the right to claim and stand on My promises without doubt, fear, or reservation. So, _____, use your personal promise book to help bring reality and clarity of My Word unto your spirit. Let My promises grow your faith, trust, and confidence in Me. My Word belongs to you. You have seen in the Bible that, on occasions, I named or renamed a place or person as a reminder of a covenant that I established with My people. Every time that name was mentioned,

7

My promise was remembered, rehearsed, and recited. So, _____, see your name, see yourself in My Word, for I have certainly made a covenant with you. When you accepted Jesus Christ and His completed work at Calvary, your name was brought before Me as a new addition to My family, as My child to whom all the privileges of My promised inheritance belong. Now receive them, receive them personally by faith.

2 Peter 1:3-4 (KJV): 3According as his divine power hath given unto us all things that pertain unto life and godliness, through the knowledge of him that hath called us to glory and virtue: 4Whereby are given unto us exceeding great and precious

PROMISES: *that by these ye might be partakers of the divine nature, having escaped the corruption that is in the world through lust.*

 AUTHORITY

_____, every believer is infused with My endless supply of power. The same power that supernaturally raised Jesus from the dead is the same power that is at work within you (Rom. 8:11). I provide the power, but you must enforce your covenant right to use My power in every aspect of your life. When you exercise your authority, I am glorified on the earth and you will walk in victory. _____, do not be deceived by the tricks and schemes of the devil. Yes, he prowls around seeking whom he can devour (1 Pet. 5:8). Those who are convinced and operating in the authority that I have provided through My Son, Jesus, cannot be devoured. The devil will bring many distractions to try to keep you spiritually weak. That is why you must build Me up big on the inside of you. My being on the inside of you will always outweigh and prevail over the devil on the outside. _____, remember that I am greater in you than he who is in the whole world (1 John 4:4)

Matthew 18:18 (KJV): ¹⁸Verily I say unto you, _____, whatsoever ye shall bind on earth shall be bound in heaven: and whatsoever ye shall loose on earth shall be loosed in heaven.

Ephesians 6:10-13 (KJV): ¹⁰Finally, my brethren, be strong in the Lord, and in the power of his might. ¹¹Put on the whole armour of God, that ye may be able to stand against the wiles of the devil. ¹²For we wrestle not against flesh and blood, but against principalities, against powers, against the rulers of the darkness of this world, against spiritual wickedness in high *places*. ¹³Wherefore take unto you the whole armour of God, that ye may be able to withstand in the evil day, and having done all, to stand.

9

Matthew 11:12 (KJV): [12]And from the days of John the Baptist until now the kingdom of heaven suffereth violence, and the violent take it by force.

2 Corinthians 10:3-5 (KJV): [3]For though we walk in the flesh, _____, we do not war after the flesh: [4](For the weapons of our warfare are not carnal, but mighty through God to the pulling down of strong holds;) [5]Casting down imaginations, and every high thing that exalteth itself against the knowledge of God, and bringing into captivity every thought to the obedience of Christ;

1 John 4:4 (KJV): [4]Ye are of God, little children, and have overcome them: because greater is he that is in you, _____, than he that is in the world.

Mark 16:17-18 (KJV): [17]And these signs shall follow them that believe; In my name shall they cast out devils; they shall speak with new tongues; 18They shall take up serpents; and if they drink any deadly thing, it shall not hurt them; they shall lay hands on the sick, and they shall recover.

Ephesians 2:6 (KJV): [6]And hath raised _us_ up together, and made us sit together in heavenly _places_ in Christ Jesus:

1 Timothy 6:12 (KJV): [12]_____, fight the good fight of faith, lay hold on eternal life, whereunto thou art also called...

Plan of Action:

_____, in order to walk in
victory you must be bold and courageous in
the authority that I have provided through the
shed blood of Jesus Christ. Jesus has already
defeated your enemy and guaranteed your
victory. Your part is just to continue to wave the
banner of victory, in the face of the enemy until
Jesus' return. Learn My Word and confess it, for
it is My Word that I look after to perform in your
life.

Confession: I take authority, in the name of
Jesus, against the powers of darkness that would
try to operate in my life-for whatever I bind
or loose on the earth, I have the agreement of
heaven that it will be done.

 BELIEF SYSTEM/BELIEVE

_____, what you believe in your heart is what you will do or act upon. Your belief system gives direction to your life. Right beliefs bring about right actions that will reap desired outcomes. If your beliefs about Me are distorted or weak, they will be unable to guide your life with absolute certainty in faith. I respond to your faith. Your belief system is that upon which true faith is built. As a believer, your belief system should be established on My Word and continually strengthened. One of weak or distorted belief will be tossed to and fro by doubt and confusion. Your belief system is the anchor for your spirit. The more you strengthen your beliefs in accordance with My Word, the deeper your anchor will settle. Believe that I am a good God and am only capable of good actions. Believe that it is My desire to bless you and all of humanity, not to harm and bring destruction. Know with all assurance that I am always here to bring you to your highest and best in every area of your life for My glory. Study My character, My position, and My abilities. Settle them in your spirit so that you will be able to distinguish My activity from that of the devil. Your belief system must be an unshakable foundation so that during the times of adversity, you will remain confident and assured of your victorious end.

Belief System

John 10:10 (KJV): ¹⁰_____, the thief cometh not, but for to steal, and to kill, and to destroy: I am come that they might have life, and that they might have *it* more abundantly.

1 John 1:5 (KJV): 5This then is the message which we have heard of him, and declare unto you, that God is light, and in him is no darkness at all.

James 1:5-8 (KJV): 5If any of you lack wisdom, let him ask of God, that giveth to all *men* liberally, and upbraideth not; and it shall be given him. 6But let him ask in faith, nothing wavering. For he that wavereth is like a wave of the sea driven with the wind and tossed. 7For let not that man think that he shall receive any thing of the Lord. 8_____, a double minded man is unstable in all his ways.

James 1:17 (KJV): 17_____, every good gift and every perfect gift is from above, and cometh down from the Father of lights, with whom is no variableness, neither shadow of turning.

Ephesians 1:3 (KJV): 3Blessed *be* the God and Father of our Lord Jesus Christ, who hath blessed us with all spiritual blessings in heavenly *place*s in Christ:

Ephesians 4:14-15 (KJV): 14That we *henceforth* be no more children, tossed to and fro, and carried about with every wind of doctrine, by the sleight of men, *and* cunning craftiness, whereby they lie in wait to deceive; 15But speaking the truth in love, may grow up into him in all things, which is the head, *even* Christ:

Ephesians 3:20 (KJV): 20Now unto him that is able to do exceeding abundantly above all that we ask or think, according to the power that worketh in us,

Acts 10:38 (KJV): 38How God anointed Jesus of Nazareth with the Holy Ghost and with power: who went about doing good, and healing all that were oppressed of the devil; for God was with him.

Romans 8:37-39 (KJV): ³⁷Nay, in all these things we are more than conquerors through him that loved us. ³⁸For I am persuaded, that neither death, nor life, nor angels, nor principalities, nor powers, nor things present, nor things to come, ³⁹Nor height, nor depth, nor any other creature, shall be able to separate us from the love of God, which is in Christ Jesus our Lord.

Philippians 4:13 (KJV): ¹³I can do all things through Christ which strengtheneth me.

Believe

John 3:16 (KJV): ¹⁶For God so loved the world, that he gave his only begotten Son, that whosoever believeth in him should not perish, but have everlasting life.

John 3:36 (KJV): ³⁶_____, he that believeth on the Son hath everlasting life: and he that believeth not the Son shall not see life; but the wrath of God abideth on him.

John 12:46 (KJV): ⁴⁶I am come a light into the world, that whosoever believeth on me should not abide in darkness.

John 6:35 (KJV): ³⁵And Jesus said unto them, I am the bread of life: he that cometh to me shall never hunger; and he that believeth on me shall never thirst.

John 6:47 (KJV): ⁴⁷Verily, verily, I say unto you, He that believeth on me hath everlasting life.

John 20:29 (KJV): ²⁹Jesus saith unto him, Thomas, because thou hast seen me, thou hast believed: blessed *are* they that have not seen, and *yet* have believed.

Romans 10:4 (KJV): [4]For Christ is the end of the law for righteousness to every one that believeth.

Mark 9:23 (KJV): [23]Jesus said unto him, If thou canst believe, *all* things are possible to him that believeth.

2 Corinthians 1:20 (KJV): [20]For all the promises of God in him are yea, and in him Amen, unto the glory of God by us.

Hebrews 13:8 (KJV): [8]Jesus Christ the same yesterday, and to day, and for ever.

Hebrews 3:18-19 (KJV): [18]And to whom sware he that they should not enter into his rest, but to them that believed not? [19]So we see that they could not enter in because of unbelief.

Hebrews 4:3 (KJV): [3]For we which have believed do enter into rest...

1 John 1:9 (KJV): [9]If we confess our sins, he is faithful and just to forgive us *our* sins, and to cleanse us from all unrighteousness

Plan of Action:

_____, settle in your heart that I am a good God and am capable of only doing good. All of My acts, thoughts and plans are good. Stop giving Me credit for the works of Satan. When the devil tries to tell you that I have done something against My nature, pull down those thoughts and bring them subject to My Word. Eventually, they will stop coming because when you draw near to Me and resist the devil, he must flee from you.

Confession: I believe and am convinced that it is the devil that comes to kill, steal, and destroy, but Jesus came that I might have life and have it full, bountiful, and plentiful.

16

 CHARACTER

_____, I know that it has been said that character is who you are when no one is looking, but I am always looking. I am looking for one who honors Me and My Spirit to the degree that he/she will control and master his/her flesh in order to have unhindered, unrestricted fellowship with Me, for My Spirit cannot dwell in an unclean vessel. Do not be deceived; the world requires that you only restrain yourself from unlawful acts, but I require an inward change. So while you may not be violating a natural law, you may be violating a spiritual law. The world says do not kill; I say do not even hate. The world says to do good only to those that are good to you, but I say to love and do good even to those that hate and mistreat you. _____, I know that you are human and at times fail to heed My Word; however, those who love Me do not remain in sin (James 3:9), but quickly repent and get back on My Spirit-led path.

2 Corinthians 4:1-2 (KJV): [1]Therefore seeing we have this ministry, as we have received mercy, we faint not; [2]But have renounced the hidden things of dishonesty, not walking in craftiness, nor handling the word of God deceitfully; but by manifestation of the truth commending ourselves to every man's conscience in the sight of God.

Galatians 5:16-17 (KJV): [16]*This* I say then, Walk in the Spirit, and ye shall not fulfil the lust of the flesh. [17]For the flesh lusteth against the Spirit, and the Spirit against the flesh: and these are contrary the one to the other: so that ye cannot do the things that ye would.

Romans 12:17 (KJV): [17]Recompense to no man evil for evil. Provide things honest in the sight of all men.

17

Luke 16:10-12 (KJV): ¹⁰He that is faithful in that which is least is faithful also in much: and he that is unjust in the least is unjust also in much. ¹¹If therefore ye have not been faithful in the unrighteous mammon, who will commit to your trust the true *riches*? ¹²And if ye have not been faithful in that which is another man's, who shall give you that which is your own?

1 Timothy 4:12 (KJV): ¹²Let no man despise thy youth; but be thou an example of the believers, in word, in conversation, in charity, in spirit, in faith, in purity.

Titus 3:1-2 (KJV): ¹Put them in mind to be subject to principalities and powers, to obey magistrates, to be ready to every good work, ²To speak evil of no man, to be no brawlers, *but* gentle, showing all meekness unto all men.

Numbers 30:2 (KJV): ²If a man vow a vow unto the LORD, or swear an oath to bind his soul with a bond; he shall not break his word, he shall do according to all that proceedeth out of his mouth.

Psalms 84:11 (KJV): ¹¹For the LORD God *is* a sun and shield: the LORD will give grace and glory: no good *thing* will he withhold from them that walk uprightly.

1 Peter 1:15-16 (KJV): ¹⁵But as he which hath called you is holy, _____, so be ye holy in all manner of conversation; ¹⁶Because it is written, Be ye holy; for I am holy.

Philippians 2:3-4 (KJV): ³*Let* nothing *be done* through strife or vainglory; but in lowliness of mind let each esteem other better than themselves. ⁴Look not every man on his own things, but every man also on the things of others.

Hebrews 12:14 (KJV): ¹⁴ _____,
Follow peace with all men, and holiness, without which
no man shall see the Lord:

James 1:22 (KJV): ²²But be ye doers of the word, and
not hearers only, deceiving your own selves.

Luke 6:45 (KJV): ⁴⁵ a good man out of the good treasure
of his heart bringeth forth that which is good; and an evil
man out of the evil treasure of his heart bringeth forth
that which is evil: for of the abundance of the heart his
mouth speaketh.

Romans 12:1-2 (KJV): ¹beseech you therefore, brethren,
by the mercies of God, that ye present your bodies a
living sacrifice, holy, acceptable unto God, _which_ is your
reasonable service. ²And be not conformed to this world:
but be ye transformed by the renewing of your mind,
that ye may prove what is that good, and acceptable, and
perfect, will of God.

2 Timothy 2:22-23 (KJV): ²²Flee also youthful lusts:
but follow righteousness, faith, charity, peace, with them
that call on the Lord out of a pure heart. ²³But foolish and
unlearned questions avoid, knowing that they do gender
strifes.

1 Thessalonians 4:3-8 (KJV): ³For this is the will of
God, _even_ your sanctification, that ye should abstain from
fornication: ⁴That every one of you should know how
to possess his vessel in sanctification and honour; ⁵Not
in the lust of concupiscence, even as the Gentiles which
know not God: ⁶That no _man_ go beyond and defraud
his brother in _any_ matter: because that the Lord is the
avenger of all such, as we also have forewarned you and
testified. ⁷For God hath not called us unto uncleanness,
but unto holiness. ⁸He therefore that despiseth, despiseth

not man, but God, who hath also given unto us his holy Spirit.

Colossians 3:8-10 (KJV): ⁸But now ye also put off all these; anger, wrath, malice, blasphemy, filthy communication out of your mouth. ⁹Lie not one to another, seeing that ye have put off the old man with his deeds; ¹⁰And have put on the new *man*, which is renewed in knowledge after the image of him that created him:

Psalms 37:23 (KJV): ²³ _____,
the steps of a *good* man are ordered by the LORD: and he delighteth in his way.

Plan of Action:

_____, search your own heart daily, repent, and turn away from those things that you know grieve My Holy Spirit on the inside of you. As you follow the leading of My Spirit, you will learn how to keep your flesh empty of the world but your spirit filled to overflow.

Confession: I am the righteousness of God in Christ Jesus, and my steps are ordered by God, for I delight in His way. I speak, act, and think in accordance with the Word of God for I desire to please my heavenly Father. I am no longer the same; I am changed, in Jesus' name.

 CONFESSION

_____, confession of sin is one side of spiritual matters and is certainly an important part of spiritual growth. However, I have already provided a complete and perfect sacrifice for all your sins through My Son, Jesus. Of great importance is your **confession of faith!** It is your confession of faith that will cause you to walk in victory here in this life. _____, many Christians have received forgiveness of sin, yet they continue to live a life of defeat, lack, and/or sickness because they have not learned that what they say does matter. Wrong confessions of defeat, weakness, lack, and failure will put one under instead of over, beneath life's circumstances instead of above them. Your confession establishes and confirms your belief. You speak your belief every time you open your mouth. Either you are speaking words that will cause My promises to manifest in your life, or that will cause the plan of Satan to manifest in your life. My promises operate on the principle of believing and confessing. First, you hear it and believe it, then you confess it out of your mouth. This is a crucial principle that must be learned, practiced and developed. This principle is distinctive of My faith-filled children. The children of the world cannot say out of their mouths with confidence that which is not made manifest. The children of the world cannot say they are rich when their bank accounts are empty, or that their body is healed when it continues to manifest the signs and symptoms of disease. That is not so with My children, for those of My family speak those things that be not as though they were. _____, you have the ability and advantage of operating in two worlds, the seen and the unseen. The seen is obvious; however you must develop yourself in the unseen, for the unseen world brings

forth the seen (Heb. 11:3). You do this by confessing My promises in the face of the seen reality.

Romans 10:8-10 (KJV): ⁸But what saith it? The word is nigh thee, *even* in thy mouth, and in thy heart: that is, the word of faith, which we preach; ⁹That if thou shalt confess with thy mouth the Lord Jesus, and shalt believe in thine heart that God hath raised him from the dead, thou shalt be saved. 10For with the heart man believeth unto righteousness; and with the mouth confession is made unto salvation.

Romans 4:17 (KJV): ¹⁷... before him whom he believed, *even* God, who quickeneth the dead, and calleth those things which be not as though they were.

2 Corinthians 4:13 (KJV): ¹³We having the same spirit of faith, according as it is written, I believed, and therefore have I spoken; we also believe, and therefore speak;

Mark 11:23-24 (KJV): ²³For verily I say unto you, That whosoever shall say unto this mountain, Be thou removed, and be thou cast into the sea; and shall not doubt in his heart, but shall believe that those things which he saith shall come to pass; he shall have whatsoever he saith. ²⁴Therefore I say unto you, What things soever ye desire, when ye pray, believe that ye receive *them,* and ye shall have *them.*

Proverbs 18:20 (KJV): ²⁰A man's belly shall be satisfied with the fruit of his mouth; *and* with the increase of his lips shall he be filled.

Proverbs 18:21 (KJV): ²¹_____,
death and life *are* in the power of the tongue: and they that love it shall eat the fruit thereof.

 Confession

John 15:7 (KJV): 7 _____, if ye abide in me, and my words abide in you, ye shall ask what ye will, and it shall be done unto you.

Matthew 12:34-37 (KJV): 34O generation of vipers, how can ye, being evil, speak good things? for out of the abundance of the heart the mouth speaketh. 35A good man out of the good treasure of the heart bringeth forth good things: and an evil man out of the evil treasure bringeth forth evil things. 36But I say unto you, That every idle word that men shall speak, they shall give account thereof in the day of judgment. 37For by thy words thou shalt be justified, and by thy words thou shalt be condemned.

1 John 5:14-15 (KJV): 14And this is the confidence that we have in him, that, if we ask any thing according to his will, he heareth us: 15And if we know that he hear us, whatsoever we ask, we know that we have the petitions that we desired of him.

Proverbs 6:2 (KJV): 2Thou art snared with the words of thy mouth, thou art taken with the words of thy mouth.

Proverbs 15:4 (KJV): 4A wholesome tongue _is_ a tree of life: but perverseness therein _is_ a breach in the spirit.

Proverbs 12:14 (KJV): 14A man shall be satisfied with good by the fruit of _his_ mouth: and the recompense of a man's hands shall be rendered unto him.

Plan of Action:

_____, developing My Word
in your spirit will change your circumstances.
Confess My Word often out of YOUR mouth so
that YOUR ears hear what YOU say. You will
soon start to believe and have faith in what you
say, and faith in My Word will surely bring your
confessions to pass.

Confession: I am healthy, wealthy, and wise. I
overcome in every area of my life by the blood of
the Lamb and the word of my testimony. I will
believe the report of the Lord concerning my life,
not the doctor, banker, or employer. I choose to
confess the works of Jesus not Satan.

- No pain, sickness, or disease can dwell in my
  body because by the stripes of Jesus, I am
  healed.

- I have no lack, and all my needs are met
  because God supplies all of my needs
  according to His riches in glory by
  Christ Jesus.

24

 FAITH

_____, faith is the key to unlocking heaven on the earth. Without faith it is impossible to please, gratify, or satisfy Me. Therefore, it is your faith that I respond to. Faith in Me is the only thing that will defeat the devil and cause you to triumph. Don't confuse mental agreement with faith. Mental agreement says it could happen. Faith says that through Jesus, it already has happened **for me!** Mental agreement is from the head, while faith is from the heart. Faith is putting action to your belief to the extent that you speak, live, and act upon it regardless of the reality of its current manifestation. Most of My promises are conditional. This means you have a part to do by faith before you experience the fulfillment of My promise. You are the only one who can and will limit My ability in your life. If you do not believe that I financially prosper My children or manifest physical healing, then you will not receive in this area of your inheritance. Whenever you limit Me, you also limit yourself from receiving My absolute best. Don't limit Me in your life, for the cup that hungers will always be filled, and those that come expecting will always get an encounter (Matt. 5:6). Allow My Word to release the restraints off of your faith.

Hebrews 11:6 (KJV): 6But without faith *it is* impossible to please *him:* for he that cometh to God must believe that he is, and *that* he is a rewarder of them that diligently seek him.

Hebrews 11:1 (KJV): 1_____, now faith is the substance of things hoped for, the evidence of things not seen.

Faith

Hebrews 10:35-38 (KJV): 35Cast not away therefore your confidence, which hath great recompense of reward. 36For ye have need of patience, that, after ye have done the will of God, ye might receive the promise. 37For yet a little while, and he that shall come will come, and will not tarry. 38Now the just shall live by faith...

Hebrews 12:2 (KJV): 2Looking unto Jesus the author and finisher of *our* faith...

Hebrews 4:2 (KJV): 2For unto us was the gospel preached, as well as unto them: but the word preached did not profit them, not being mixed with faith in them that heard *it.*

Hebrews 10:23 (KJV): 23_____, let us hold fast the profession of *our* faith without wavering; (for he is faithful that promised;)

2 Corinthians 5:7 (KJV): 7(For we walk by faith, not by sight:)

2 Corinthians 4:13 (KJV): 13We having the same spirit of faith, according as it is written, I believed, and therefore have I spoken; we also believe, and therefore speak;

Matthew 9:21-22 (KJV): 21For she said within herself, If I may but touch his garment, I shall be whole. 22But Jesus turned him about, and when he saw her, he said, Daughter, be of good comfort; thy faith hath made thee whole. And the woman was made whole from that hour.

Matthew 19:26 (KJV): 26But Jesus beheld *them,* and said unto them, With men this is impossible; but with God all things are possible.

Mark 9:23 (KJV): 23Jesus said unto him, If thou canst believe, all things *are* possible to him that believeth.

Faith

Mark 11:22-24 (KJV): ²²And Jesus answering saith unto them, Have faith in God. ²³For verily I say unto you, That whosoever shall say unto this mountain, Be thou removed, and be thou cast into the sea; and shall not doubt in his heart, but shall believe that those things which he saith shall come to pass; he shall have whatsoever he saith. ²⁴Therefore I say unto you, What things soever ye desire, when ye pray, believe that ye receive *them*, and ye shall have *them*.

1 Timothy 6:12 (KJV): ¹²Fight the good fight of faith, lay hold on eternal life, whereunto thou art also called, and hast professed a good profession before many witnesses.

Habakkuk 2:4 (KJV): ⁴Behold, his soul *which* is lifted up is not upright in him: but the just shall live by his faith.

Romans 1:17 (KJV): ¹⁷For therein is the righteousness of God revealed from faith to faith: as it is written, The just shall live by faith.

Romans 4:17 (KJV): ¹⁷...before him whom he believed, *even* God, who quickeneth the dead, and calleth those things which be not as though they were.

Romans 10:17 (KJV): ¹⁷So then faith *cometh* by hearing, and hearing by the word of God.

James 1:5-8 (KJV): ⁵If any of you lack wisdom, let him ask of God, that giveth to all *men* liberally, and upbraideth not; and it shall be given him. ⁶But let him ask in faith, nothing wavering. For he that wavereth is like a wave of the sea driven with the wind and tossed. ⁷For let not that man think that he shall receive any thing of the Lord. ⁸A double minded man *is* unstable in all his ways.

Ephesians 2:8 (KJV): 8_____,
for by grace are ye saved through faith; and that not of
yourselves: *it is* the gift of God:

Galatians 2:20 (KJV): 20I am crucified with Christ:
nevertheless I live; yet not I, but Christ liveth in me: and
the life which I now live in the flesh I live by the faith of
the Son of God, who loved me, and gave himself for me.

Galatians 3:26 (KJV): 26_____, for
ye are all the children of God by faith in Christ Jesus.

Galatians 3:11 (KJV): 11But that no man is justified by
the law in the sight of God, *it is* evident: for, the just shall
live by faith.

28

Galatians 3:14 (KJV): 14That the blessing of Abraham
might come on the Gentiles through Jesus Christ; that we
might receive the promise of the Spirit through faith.

Galatians 3:6-9 (KJV): 6Even as Abraham believed
God, and it was accounted to him for righteousness. 7Know
ye therefore that they which are of faith, the same are the
children of Abraham. 8And the scripture, foreseeing that
God would justify the heathen through faith, preached
before the gospel unto Abraham, *saying,* In thee shall all
nations be blessed. 9So then they which be of faith are
blessed with faithful Abraham.

1 Peter 1:7 (KJV): 7That the trial of your faith, being
much more precious than of gold that perisheth, though it
be tried with fire, might be found unto praise and honour
and glory at the appearing of Jesus Christ:

1 John 5:4 (KJV): 4_____, for
whatsoever is born of God overcometh the world: and this
is the victory that overcometh the world, *even* our faith.

Faith

Plan of Action:

_____, faith moves you from mental assent to trusting in Me and acting upon My Word. Stop hoping that I will, and know that I already have. Understanding WHY you do is not a requirement of faith, but DOING is. So when things seem hard and you're going through hardships and you don't know what you're going to do, walk by faith and not by sight and I will see you through.

Confession: I have faith and speak those things that are not as though they were, and they shall come to pass.

 FAMILY/MARRIAGE/UNITY/CHILDREN

_____, the family unit is very important to Me, especially the marriage covenant, for I am a God of covenant. Marriage is a representation of the unconditional covenant relationship that Jesus has with the church. The family unit is intended to be the primary institution of love, learning, and instructing in My way. The intimate love relationship that should exist between the members of the family sets the stage for one to have the proper perspective of My love and the love toward others. The degree that one has experienced My love through the family is the degree that one will be able to express and receive love (1 Cor. 13) _____, I have laid out specific promises and standards for each member of the family in My Word. So choose to be a doer of My Word to secure the success of your family, and the end result will surely be *"happily everafter."*

Family/Marriage/Unity

Amos 3:3 (KJV): [3]Can two walk together, except they be agreed?

Matthew 12:25 (KJV): [25]And Jesus knew their thoughts, and said unto them, Every kingdom divided against itself is brought to desolation; and every city or house divided against itself shall not stand:

Matthew 18:19-20 (KJV): [19]Again I say unto you, That if two of you shall agree on earth as touching any thing that they shall ask, it shall be done for them of my Father which is in heaven. [20]For where two or three are gathered together in my name, there am I in the midst of them.

Philippians 2:2-3 (KJV): ²Fulfil ye my joy, that ye be likeminded, having the same love, *being* of one accord, of one mind. ³*Let* nothing *be done* through strife or vainglory; but in lowliness of mind let each esteem other better than themselves.

1 Timothy 3:3-5 (KJV): ³Not given to wine, no striker, not greedy of filthy lucre; but patient, not a brawler, not covetous; ⁴One that ruleth well his own house, having his children in subjection with all gravity; ⁵(For if a man know not how to rule his own house, how shall he take care of the church of God?)

Titus 2:3-5 (KJV): ³The aged women likewise, that *they be* in behaviour as becometh holiness, not false accusers, not given to much wine, teachers of good things; ⁴That they may teach the young women to be sober, to love their husbands, to love their children, ⁵*To be* discreet, chaste, keepers at home, good, obedient to their own husbands, that the word of God be not blasphemed.

Galatians 6:2 (KJV): ²_____, bear ye one another's burdens, and so fulfill the law of Christ.

1 Corinthians 7:1-5 (KJV): ¹*It is* good for a man not to touch a woman. ²Nevertheless, *to avoid* fornication, let every man have his own wife, and let every woman have her own husband. ³Let the husband render unto the wife due benevolence: and likewise also the wife unto the husband. ⁴The wife hath not power of her own body, but the husband: and likewise also the husband hath not power of his own body, but the wife. ⁵Defraud ye not one the other, except *it be* with consent for a time, that ye may give yourselves to fasting and prayer; and come together again, that Satan tempt you not for your incontinency.

Hebrews 13:4 (KJV): ⁴Marriage *is* honourable in all, and the bed undefiled: but whoremongers and adulterers God will judge.

Ephesians 5:21-33 (KJV): ²¹Submitting yourselves one to another in the fear of God. ²²Wives, submit yourselves unto your own husbands, as unto the Lord. ²³For the husband is the head of the wife, even as Christ is the head of the church: and he is the saviour of the body. ²⁴Therefore as the church is subject unto Christ, so *let* the wives *be* to their own husbands in every thing. ²⁵Husbands, love your wives, even as Christ also loved the church, and gave himself for it; ²⁶That he might sanctify and cleanse it with the washing of water by the word, ²⁷That he might present it to himself a glorious church, not having spot, or wrinkle, or any such thing; but that it should be holy and without blemish. ²⁸So ought men to love their wives as their own bodies. He that loveth his wife loveth himself. ²⁹For no man ever yet hated his own flesh; but nourisheth and cherisheth it, even as the Lord the church: ³⁰For we are members of his body, of his flesh, and of his bones. ³¹For this cause shall a man leave his father and mother, and shall be joined unto his wife, and they two shall be one flesh. ³²This is a great mystery: but I speak concerning Christ and the church. ³³Nevertheless let every one of you in particular so love his wife even as himself; and the wife see that she reverence *her* husband.

Psalms 78:4-7 (KJV): ⁴We will not hide *them* from their children, showing to the generation to come the praises of the LORD, and his strength, and his wonderful works that he hath done. ⁵For he established a testimony in Jacob, and appointed a law in Israel, which he commanded our fathers, that they should make them known to their children: ⁶That the generation to come might know *them, even* the children *which* should be born; *who* should arise and declare *them* to their children: ⁷That they might set their hope in God, and not forget the works of God, but keep his commandments:

Psalms 133:1 (KJV): ¹ Behold, how good and how pleasant *it is* for brethren to dwell together in unity!

Proverbs 18:22 (KJV): ²²*Whoso* findeth a wife findeth a good *thing,* and obtaineth favour of the LORD.

Proverbs 31:10-12 (KJV): ¹⁰Who can find a virtuous woman? for her price is far above rubies. ¹¹The heart of her husband doth safely trust in her, so that he shall have no need of spoil. ¹²She will do him good and not evil all the days of her life.

Ecclesiastes 4:9-12 (KJV): ⁹_____, two *are* better than one; because they have a good reward for their labour. 10For if they fall, the one will lift up his fellow: but woe to him *that is* alone when he falleth; for *he hath* not another to help him up. ¹¹Again, if two lie together, then they have heat: but how can one be warm *alone?* ¹²And if one prevail against him, two shall withstand him; and a threefold cord is not quickly broken.

33

Children

Ephesians 6:1-4 (KJV): ¹Children, obey your parents in the Lord: for this is right. ²Honour thy father and mother; (which is the first commandment with promise;) ³That it may be well with thee, and thou mayest live long on the earth. ⁴And, ye fathers, provoke not your children to wrath: but bring them up in the nurture and admonition of the Lord.

Colossians 3:20 (KJV): ²⁰Children, obey *your* parents in all things: for this is well pleasing unto the Lord.

Mark 10:14-16 (KJV): ¹⁴But when Jesus saw *it,* he was much displeased, and said unto them, Suffer the little children to come unto me, and forbid them not: for of such is the kingdom of God. ¹⁵Verily I say unto you,

Whosoever shall not receive the kingdom of God as a little child, he shall not enter therein. 16And he took them up in his arms, put *his* hands upon them, and blessed them.

Isaiah 54:13 (KJV): 13And all thy children *shall be* taught of the LORD; and great *shall be* the peace of thy children.

Psalms 128:3 (KJV): 3 Thy wife *shall be* as a fruitful vine by the sides of thine house: thy children like olive plants round about thy table.

Proverbs 17:6 (KJV): 6Children's children *are* the crown of old men; and the glory of children *are* their fathers.

Proverbs 22:15 (KJV): 15Foolishness *is* bound in the heart of a child; *but* the rod of correction shall drive it far from him.

Proverbs 19:18 (KJV): 18Chasten thy son while there is hope, and let not thy soul spare for his crying.

Proverbs 13:1 (KJV): 1A wise son *heareth* his father's instruction: but a scorner heareth not rebuke.

Proverbs 13:24 (KJV): 24He that spareth his rod hateth his son: but he that loveth him chasteneth him betimes.

Proverbs 23:24-26 (KJV): 24The father of the righteous shall greatly rejoice: and he that begetteth a wise *child* shall have joy of him. 25Thy father and thy mother shall be glad, and she that bare thee shall rejoice. 26My son, give me thine heart, and let thine eyes observe my ways.

Isaiah 54:13 (KJV): 13And all thy children *shall be* taught of the LORD; and great *shall be* the peace of thy children.

34

Plan of Action:

_____, be an accountable and responsible member of your family. Study My Word to find out the responsibilities of your position and role in your family. Prayer and your godly lifestyle are the keys to effective change in your family. Don't get discouraged by what you currently see, for I am working behind the scenes on the heart of each family member that you have committed to Me in prayer.

Confession: My family represents the covenant and unity of God on the earth. We walk in forgiveness, oneness, and love.

 FORGIVENESS (BROTHERLY/GOD'S)

_____, there is freedom in the grace of forgiveness. I have chosen to express Myself to the world through forgiveness and love. I desire for My children to follow My example. When you choose to forgive, you release yourself and the one forgiven to live a life of freedom. From the very moment of Adam's sin in the garden, I have been unfolding My plan of forgiveness toward mankind. Everything that I have done, everything that My Son, Jesus, did, and everything that the Holy Spirit is now doing is to redeem you and all of humanity from the sin nature that separates us. Forgiveness is the core of My kingdom to demonstrate My love and plan on the earth. Forgiveness is-on going; you must be determined to walk in forgiveness daily in order for the flow of forgiveness to continue to operate on your behalf.

36

Forgiveness (Brotherly)

Matthew 6:14-15 (KJV): [14]For if ye forgive men their trespasses, _____, your heavenly Father will also forgive you: [15]But if ye forgive not men their trespasses, neither will your Father forgive your trespasses.

Matthew 5:44-45 (KJV): [44]But I say unto you, Love your enemies, bless them that curse you, do good to them that hate you, and pray for them which despitefully use you, and persecute you; [45]That ye may be the children of your Father which is in heaven: for he maketh his sun to rise on the evil and on the good, and sendeth rain on the just and on the unjust.

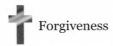

Mark 11:24-26 (KJV): ²⁴Therefore I say unto you, What things soever ye desire, when ye pray, believe that ye receive *them*, and ye shall have *them*. ²⁵And when ye stand praying, forgive, if ye have ought against any: that your Father also which is in heaven may forgive you your trespasses. ²⁶But if ye do not forgive, neither will your Father which is in heaven forgive your trespasses.

Romans 12:16-21 (KJV): ¹⁶*Be* of the same mind one toward another. Mind not high things, but condescend to men of low estate. Be not wise in your own conceits. ¹⁷Recompense to no man evil for evil. Provide things honest in the sight of all men. ¹⁸If it be possible, as much as lieth in you, live peaceably with all men. ¹⁹Dearly beloved, avenge not yourselves, but *rather* give place unto wrath: for it is written, Vengeance is mine; I will repay, saith the Lord. ²⁰Therefore if thine enemy hunger, feed him; if he thirst, give him drink: for in so doing thou shalt heap coals of fire on his head. ²¹Be not overcome of evil, but overcome evil with good.

37

Luke 6:35-37 (KJV): ³⁵But love ye your enemies, and do good, and lend, hoping for nothing again; and your reward shall be great, and ye shall be the children of the Highest: for he is kind unto the unthankful and *to* the evil. ³⁶_____, be ye therefore merciful, as your Father also is merciful. ³⁷Judge not, and ye shall not be judged: condemn not, and ye shall not be condemned: forgive, and ye shall be forgiven:

Colossians 3:13 (KJV): ¹³Forbearing one another, and forgiving one another, _____, if any man have a quarrel against any: even as Christ forgave you, so also *do ye*.

Matthew 18:21-22 (KJV): ²¹Then came Peter to him, and said, Lord, how oft shall my brother sin against me,

and I forgive him? till seven times? ²²Jesus saith unto him, I say not unto thee, Until seven times: but, Until seventy times seven.

Luke 17:3-4 (KJV): ³Take heed to yourselves: If thy brother trespass against thee, rebuke him; and if he repent, forgive him. ⁴And if he trespass against thee seven times in a day, and seven times in a day turn again to thee, saying, I repent; thou shalt forgive him.

Proverbs 20:22 (KJV): ²²Say not thou, I will recompense evil; *but* wait on the LORD, and he shall save thee.

38

Forgiveness (God's)

Psalms 32:1-2 (KJV): ¹Blessed *is he whose* transgression *is* forgiven, *whose* sin *is* covered. ²Blessed is the man unto whom the LORD imputeth not iniquity, and in whose spirit *there is* no guile.

2 Corinthians 5:19 (KJV): ¹⁹To wit, that God was in Christ, reconciling the world unto himself, not imputing their trespasses unto them; and hath committed unto us the word of reconciliation.

Hebrews 8:12 (KJV): ¹²For I will be merciful to their unrighteousness, and their sins and their iniquities will I remember no more.

Romans 8:1-3 (KJV): ¹*There* is therefore now no condemnation to them which are in Christ Jesus, who walk not after the flesh, but after the Spirit. ²For the law of the Spirit of life in Christ Jesus hath made me free from the law of sin and death. ³For what the law could not do, in that it was weak through the flesh, God sending his own

Son in the likeness of sinful flesh, and for sin, condemned sin in the flesh:

1 John 1:9 (KJV): [9]If we confess our sins, he is faithful and just to forgive us *our* sins, and to cleanse us from all unrighteousness.

Isaiah 43:25 (KJV): [25]I, *even I, am* he that blotteth out thy transgressions for mine own sake, and will not remember thy sins.

Psalms 103:8 (KJV): [8]The LORD is merciful and gracious, slow to anger, and plenteous in mercy.

Plan of Action:

_____, just receive My forgiveness, knowing that I have made provision for all of your sins, emotional weaknesses, and personality flaws through Jesus Christ. Don't allow anger, pain, or frustration to hinder you from forgiving others. Just remember all that is *"wrapped"* up in your forgiveness of others, the *'gift'* of My grace and forgiveness flowing through and for your life daily.

Confession: Freely I receive the forgiveness of God; freely I forgive others.

 (YOUR) FUTURE

_____, though you exist in the
natural, the true significance of your existence is spiritual
and eternal. There is so much more to your life than the
physical and the natural! _____,
you can trust Me with every entity of your life. I have a
view of your life that you do not, for I see and know the
end from the beginning. My plans for you are always
good. My plans are always to bless and not to curse,
to increase and never to take away. I will always do
exceedingly, abundantly more than you could have ever
thought, dreamed, or imagined possible with your life.
_____, remember that he who tries
to save his life or live his life according to his own plans
will lose it or get less than he planned. However, he who
loses his life to and for Me, or gives himself and his plans
completely to Me, will gain his life and get more than he
planned.

Jeremiah 29:11 (KJV): [11]_____,
for I know the thoughts that I think toward you, saith the
LORD, thoughts of peace, and not of evil, to give you an
expected end.

Isaiah 46:10 (KJV): [10]Declaring the end from the
beginning, and from ancient times *the things* that are not
yet done, saying, My counsel shall stand, and I will do all
my pleasure:

Matthew 10:39 (KJV): [39]He that findeth his life shall
lose it: and he that loseth his life for my sake shall find it.

Colossians 3:2-4 (KJV): [2]_____,
set your affection on things above, not on things on the
earth. [3]For ye are dead, and your life is hid with Christ

40

in God. ⁴When Christ, *who is* our life, shall appear, then shall ye also appear with him in glory.

Hebrews 12:1-2 (KJV): ¹Wherefore seeing we also are compassed about with so great a cloud of witnesses, let us lay aside every weight, and the sin which doth so easily beset *us,* and let us run with patience the race that is set before us, ²Looking unto Jesus the author and finisher of *our* faith; who for the joy that was set before him endured the cross, despising the shame, and is set down at the right hand of the throne of God.

1 John 2:23-25 (KJV): ²³_____, whosoever denieth the Son, the same hath not the Father: *(but) he that acknowledgeth the Son hath the Father also.* ²⁴Let that therefore abide in you, which ye have heard from the beginning. If that which ye have heard from the beginning shall remain in you, ye also shall continue in the Son, and in the Father. ²⁵And this is the promise that he hath promised us, *even* eternal life.

Romans 8:18 (KJV): ¹⁸For I reckon that the sufferings of this present time *are* not worthy *to be compared* with the glory which shall be revealed in us.

2 Corinthians 5:17 (KJV): ¹⁷Therefore if any man *be* in Christ, *he is* a new creature: old things are passed away; behold, all things are become new.

Philippians 1:6 (KJV): ⁶Being confident of this very thing, that he which hath begun a good work in you will perform *it* until the day of Jesus Christ:

1 Thessalonians 5:23-24 (KJV): ²³And the very God of peace sanctify you wholly; and *I pray God* your whole spirit and soul and body be preserved blameless unto the coming of our Lord Jesus Christ. ²⁴Faithful is he that calleth you, who also will do *it.*

John 14:1-3 (KJV): ¹Let not your heart be troubled: ye believe in God, believe also in me. ²In my Father's house are many mansions: if *it were* not *so,* I would have told you. I go to prepare a place for you. ³And if I go and prepare a place for you, I will come again, and receive you unto myself; that where I am, *there* ye may be also.

Revelation 3:21 (KJV): ²¹To him that overcometh will I grant to sit with me in my throne, even as I also overcame, and am set down with my Father in his throne.

Revelation 12:11 (KJV): ¹¹And they overcame him by the blood of the Lamb, and by the word of their testimony; and they loved not their lives unto the death.

42

Plan of Action:

_____, decide to live your life for Me knowing that I consider the end of your life from the beginning of your life. I know your potential and the plan that I have for you before you were even conceived. I know what will bring you fulfillment and happiness. That which is unknown to you is known to Me because I created you. Therefore, allow Me to lead you before making life-changing decisions that have unknown outcomes and I will lead you in the way that is guaranteed victorious and successful.

Confession: I give myself wholly to the Father, laying aside what I want for what He wants for me. My future is prosperous and bright because I choose to be led by the Holy Spirit and walk in His light.

GOD'S HOLY WORD

_____, there is life and liberty in My Word. My Word is active and powerful. The **action** of My Word brought forth the whole universe and everything in it. The action of My Word became flesh! _____, the truth is, I and My Word are one and cannot be separated. I am the fullness of My Word. My Word, though similar, is superior to a contract or a legal agreement; it is a covenant. A contract is an agreement between two parties that holds each responsible for fulfilling his portion of the agreement. The relationship between the parties usually resolves when either the agreement is fulfilled or one of the parties breaks or violates the agreement. That is not so with My covenant. My covenant is not based on the other party. The covenant that I instituted is by Me, agreed upon with Me and therefore based solely on Me, for when I could find no one greater to swear by, I swore by Myself in order to consummate My covenant. The other party not doing its part does not nullify the covenant; it just keeps the other party from receiving the benefits of the covenant. My covenant is from everlasting to everlasting. My Holy Word is the written form of the covenant that I established for, you, My child before the foundation of the earth. Though I am sovereign, I hold Myself accountable to My Word. I am a fair and just God, and My covenant is the standard of My equality and justice; therefore, I will not and cannot violate it. My supernatural power is not released on your behalf because of pity or race or gender or financial status. FAITH is what unleashes the reality of My Word into your life and this is the requirement for everyone who comes to Me. Many question why I would allow certain things to happen on the earth or to certain people. Well, because I will not violate My Word, I cannot stop it. The fulfillment of My covenant cost My only Son

43

his life. I could not violate My Word to spare Jesus from persecution. If I violate My covenant even one time, it nullifies the entire covenant. I have promised that not one word of My covenant will fall to the ground and that every word that I have spoken will be fulfilled and come to pass. My Word is given to you to build faith in your heart so that you will take your God-given authority and exercise it upon the earth. It reveals your heavenly inheritance and the promises, terms, and conditions of the covenant that I have made with you. Therefore, make it a priority to study, meditate on, and be a doer of My Word.

John 1:1 (KJV): 1_____, in the beginning was the Word, and the Word was with God, and the Word was God.

John 1:14 (KJV): 14And the Word was made flesh, and dwelt among us, (and we beheld his glory, the glory as of the only begotten of the Father,) full of grace and truth.

Mark 16:20 (KJV): 20And they went forth, and preached every where, the Lord working with *them,* and confirming the word with signs following. Amen.

Matthew 4:4 (KJV): 4But he answered and said, It is written, Man shall not live by bread alone, but by every word that proceedeth out of the mouth of God.

Colossians 3:16 (KJV): 16_____, let the word of Christ dwell in you richly in all wisdom; teaching and admonishing one another in psalms and hymns and spiritual songs, singing with grace in your hearts to the Lord.

Hebrews 4:12 (KJV): 12For the word of God is quick, and powerful, and sharper than any twoedged sword, piercing even to the dividing asunder of soul and spirit,

and of the joints and marrow, and is a discerner of the thoughts and intents of the heart.

James 1:21-25 (KJV): ²¹Wherefore lay apart all filthiness and superfluity of naughtiness, and receive with meekness the engrafted word, which is able to save your souls. ²²But be ye doers of the word, and not hearers only, deceiving your own selves. ²³For if any be a hearer of the word, and not a doer, he is like unto a man beholding his natural face in a glass: ²⁴For he beholdeth himself, and goeth his way, and straightway forgetteth what manner of man he was. ²⁵But whoso looketh into the perfect law of liberty, and continueth *therein,* he being not a forgetful hearer, but a doer of the work, this man shall be blessed in his deed.

45

Romans 10:17 (KJV): ¹⁷So then faith *cometh* by hearing, and hearing by the word of God.

John 6:68 (KJV): ⁶⁸Then Simon Peter answered him, Lord, to whom shall we go? thou hast the words of eternal life.

John 15:7 (KJV): ⁷_____, if ye abide in me, and my words abide in you, ye shall ask what ye will, and it shall be done unto you.

1 John 2:14 (KJV): ¹⁴..._____, the word of God abideth in you, and ye have overcome the wicked one.

2 Timothy 2:15 (KJV): ¹⁵_____, study to show thyself approved unto God, a workman that needeth not to be ashamed, rightly dividing the word of truth.

1 Peter 1:23 (KJV): [23]Being born again, not of corruptible seed, but of incorruptible, by the word of God, which liveth and abideth for ever.

Revelation 1:3 (KJV): [3]Blessed *is* he that readeth, and they that hear the words of this prophecy, and keep those things which are written therein: for the time *is* at hand.

Hosea 4:6 (KJV): [6]My people are destroyed for lack of knowledge: because thou hast rejected knowledge, I will also reject thee, that thou shalt be no priest to me: seeing thou hast forgotten the law of thy God, I will also forget thy children.

46

Deuteronomy 8:3 (KJV): [3]And he humbled thee, and suffered thee to hunger, and fed thee with manna, which thou knewest not, neither did thy fathers know; that he might make thee know that man doth not live by bread only, but by every *word* that proceedeth out of the mouth of the LORD doth man live.

Deuteronomy 11:18 (KJV): [18]Therefore shall ye lay up these my words in your heart and in your soul, and bind them for a sign upon your hand, that they may be as frontlets between your eyes.

Psalms 119:130 (KJV): [130] The entrance of thy words giveth light; it giveth understanding unto the simple.

Psalms 119:103-104 (KJV): [103] How sweet are thy words unto my taste! *yea, sweeter* than honey to my mouth! [104] Through thy precepts I get understanding: therefore I hate every false way.

Psalms 107:20 (KJV): [20]He sent his word, and healed them, and delivered *them* from their destructions.

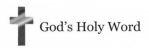

Psalms 12:6 (KJV): ⁶The words of the LORD *are* pure words: *as* silver tried in a furnace of earth, purified seven times.

Psalms 119:89 (KJV): ⁸⁹For ever, O LORD, thy word is settled in heaven.

Psalms 119:105 (KJV): ¹⁰⁵Thy word *is* a lamp unto my feet, and a light unto my path.

> ### *Plan of Action:*
>
> _____, I do not respond to the devil's word; I do not respond to your words of murmuring and complaining. I respond to My Word. So meditate on My Word day and night. _____, ultimately, be a doer of My Word and not a hearer only. A hearer knows My Word and often-times has even committed it to memory. But a doer knows My Word and has committed it to his heart/spirit. A hearer knows what I have said, but lacks the faith to *act upon* it. A doer knows My Word, receives My Word as truth and acts upon My Word by faith. Your acting upon My Word will never, ever fail.
>
> **Confession:** I hold fast to the Word of God. I live according to the Word of God. I can be, I can do, and I can have what my covenant says I can!

 *GUARD YOUR MIND*

_____, your mind is the place where Satan tries to enter your life. He comes with negativity, thoughts of fear, anger, jealousy, covetousness, lust, and the like. You must learn to pull down these thoughts and dominate them from your spirit with My Word- for, _____, though you walk in the flesh, the weapons that you fight with are not carnal, but mighty in Me for the pulling down of strongholds, even thoughts. _____, if you can control your thoughts, you will be able to control what you feel, what you do, and how you live. This is how you defeat depression and oppression. Depression and oppression manifest because of a lack of spiritual dominance. One that is depressed or oppressed has looped thoughts from the devil over and over again in his head until these thoughts become his reality. Do not be deceived. Those silent conversations that you carry out in your head are not just a natural occurrence. Most of the time, this is the beginning of a spiritual attack, in which Satan is trying to lay the foundational structure of a stronghold in your life. Satan is always trying to talk with you in your head because he cannot take hold of you in your spirit. When the Holy Spirit brings a Word to your spirit, Satan immediately comes to contradict it with thoughts of fear, reasoning, and doubt (Matt. 13:19). _____, you were created to be spirit-dominant, not mind-dominant. However, most believers have never learned how to dominate their mind from their spirit. You must *train* yourself to be spirit-dominant. You accomplish this by thinking and living according to My Word. When Satan brings thoughts to your mind that are contrary to My Word, do not hold mental conversations with him. *You* can and will defeat him if *you* would immediately open your mouth and speak My Word back at him!

Isaiah 61:3 (KJV): ³To appoint unto them that mourn in Zion, to give unto them beauty for ashes, the oil of joy for mourning, the garment of praise for the spirit of heaviness; that they might be called trees of righteousness, the planting of the LORD, that he might be glorified.

Isaiah 26:3 (KJV): ³Thou wilt keep *him* in perfect peace, *whose* mind is stayed **on thee:** because he trusteth in thee.

Philippians 4:7-8 (KJV): ⁷And the peace of God, which passeth all understanding, shall keep your hearts and minds through Christ Jesus. ⁸Finally, brethren, whatsoever things are true, whatsoever things *are* honest, whatsoever things *are* just, whatsoever things *are* pure, whatsoever things *are* lovely, whatsoever things *are* of good report; if *there* be any virtue, and if *there* be any praise, think on these things.

Romans 8:5-6 (KJV): ⁵For they that are after the flesh do mind the things of the flesh; but they that are after the Spirit the things of the Spirit. ⁶For to be carnally minded *is* death; but to be spiritually minded *is* life and peace.

Romans 12:2 (KJV): ²And be not conformed to this world: but be ye transformed by the renewing of your mind, that ye may prove what is that good, and acceptable, and perfect, will of God.

Philippians 2:5 (KJV): ⁵Let this mind be in you, which was also in Christ Jesus:

2 Corinthians 10:5 (KJV): ⁵Casting down imaginations, and every high thing that exalteth itself against the knowledge of God, and bringing into captivity every thought to the obedience of Christ;

Proverbs 23:7 (KJV): [7]For as he thinketh in his heart, so *is* he:...

Proverbs 12:5 (KJV): [5]The thoughts of the righteous *are* right: *but* the counsels of the wicked *are* deceit.

Plan of Action:

_____, as a man thinks so is he, so think on those things that are true, honest, pure, lovely, praiseworthy, and of a good report.   Resist the pull of Satan and the world by feeding your spirit with My Word and starving your mind of thoughts and words that contradict My Word.

Confession: My mind is renewed by the Word of God and I pull down and take authority over those thoughts that are contrary to the Word of God.

 HEALING

_____, My Word is healing for your spirit, soul, and body. It is easy for most to believe that I heal the spirit, but many have difficulty believing that I heal the body. Even believers have come up with reasons why pain, sickness, and disease are from Me, authorized by Me, and used by Me. Well, I do not give it, authorize it, or use it. I do not get in cahoots with the devil and the powers of darkness to accomplish My plans in the lives of My children (Matt. 12:25-30). Nor do I use sickness and disease to teach My children a lesson. I did not provide any pain, sickness, or disease when I created the earth, so I did not intend for it to be upon the earth. It came with the fall of humanity. It is apart of the curse, but Jesus has redeemed you from the curse. While Jesus lived on the earth, you find no accounts of him giving anyone pain, sickness or disease, only taking it away. Well, physical healing was not just for those who had the opportunity to reap the benefit of Jesus' presence. I did not start healing at the beginning of My Word only to take it out at the end of the book of Revelation-for My timeframe concerning My Word is only forever and everlasting. I do not change, and so it does not change. Jesus, being one Person, could only heal a few that He came in contact with while He was on the earth. Well, now, because of the Holy Spirit, all believers have access to that same healing virtue that Jesus dispensed to everyone that came to Him in faith. Jesus' completed work at Calvary is sufficient to undo whatever Satan has brought against you in every area of your life, including healing for your body.

Acts 10:38 (KJV): 38How God anointed Jesus of Nazareth with the Holy Ghost and with power: who went about doing good, and healing all that were oppressed of the devil; for God was with him.

51

Isaiah 53:4-5 (KJV): [4]Surely he hath borne our griefs, and carried our sorrows: yet we did esteem him stricken, smitten of God, and afflicted. [5]But he *was* wounded for our transgressions, *he was* bruised for our iniquities: the chastisement of our peace *was* upon him; and with his stripes we are healed.

Luke 4:18-19 (KJV): [18]The Spirit of the Lord *is* upon me, because he hath anointed me to preach the gospel to the poor; he hath sent me to heal the brokenhearted, to preach deliverance to the captives, and recovering of sight to the blind, to set at liberty them that are bruised, [19]To preach the acceptable year of the Lord.

John 10:10 (KJV): [10]_____, the thief cometh not, but for to steal, and to kill, and to destroy: I am come that they might have life, and that they might have *it* more abundantly.

Mark 10:27 (KJV): [27]And Jesus looking upon them saith, With men *it is* impossible, but not with God: for with God all things are possible.

Mark 16:18 (KJV): [18]They shall take up serpents; and if they drink any deadly thing, it shall not hurt them; they shall lay hands on the sick, and they shall recover.

Matthew 8:17 (KJV): [17]That it might be fulfilled which was spoken by Esaias the prophet, saying, Himself took our infirmities, and bare *our* sicknesses.

Hebrews 2:14-15 (KJV): [14]Forasmuch then as the children are partakers of flesh and blood, he also himself likewise took part of the same; that through death he might destroy him that had the power of death, that is, the devil; [15]And deliver them who through fear of death were all their lifetime subject to bondage.

1 Peter 2:24 (KJV): ²⁴Who his own self bare our sins in his own body on the tree, that we, being dead to sins, should live unto righteousness: by whose stripes ye were healed.

Psalms 103:3 (KJV): ³ Who forgiveth all thine iniquities; who healeth all thy diseases;

Psalms 107:20 (KJV): ²⁰He sent his word, and healed them, and delivered *them* from their destructions.

Plan of Action:

_____, daily strengthen your belief in My healing power. Speak My Word whenever Satan tries to manifest pain, sickness, or disease in your body. Ask yourself, "Whose report will I believe? Whose report do I have more trust and confidence in?" Strengthen yourself in My Word until the answer is always a resounding "The Lord's!" (Isa. 53:1)

Confession: Jesus bore my sickness on the cross that I not have to. Therefore, I believe the report of the Lord, and His report says I AM HEALED by the stripes of Jesus!

 HOLY SPIRIT

_____, I am a triune being, or three totally different and unique personalities but one completely unified Spirit. The Holy Spirit is the third Person of the Trinity and the last manifestation of Me on the earth until the return of Jesus. Just as Jesus is a Person, so is the Holy Spirit. He is here to do something, to say something, and to accomplish My plan and purpose on the earth. The Holy Spirit is actively at work in the church and in the lives of believers. He is My means of expression, operation, and demonstration in your life. It is the Holy Spirit on the inside of you who maintains your heavenly connection. It is the Holy Spirit who causes My children to be the salt and light of the world. It is the Holy Spirit that demonstrates My power and love through believers upon the earth. My children are not led by natural thinking and knowledge or feelings of the flesh. My children are led supernaturally by the Holy Spirit.

John 20:22 (KJV): ²²And when he had said this, he breathed on them, and saith unto *them,* Receive ye the Holy Ghost:

Luke 11:13 (KJV): ¹³If ye then, being evil, know how to give good gifts unto *your* children: how much more shall *your* heavenly Father give the Holy Spirit to them that ask him?

1 Corinthians 2:10-11 (KJV): ¹⁰But God hath revealed *them* unto us by his Spirit: for the Spirit searcheth all things, yea, the deep things of God. ¹¹For what man knoweth the things of a man, save the spirit of man which is in him? even so the things of God knoweth no man, but the Spirit of God.

Acts 2:4 (KJV): ⁴And they were all filled with the Holy Ghost, and began to speak with other tongues, as the Spirit gave them utterance.

Acts 5:32 (KJV): ³²And we are his witnesses of these things; and so *is* also the Holy Ghost, whom God hath given to them that obey him.

John 6:63 (KJV): ⁶³It is the spirit that quickeneth; the flesh profiteth nothing: the words that I speak unto you, *they* are spirit, and *they* are life.

John 14:16-17 (KJV): ¹⁶And I will pray the Father, and he shall give you another Comforter, that he may abide with you for ever; ¹⁷*Even* the Spirit of truth; whom the world cannot receive, because it seeth him not, neither knoweth him: but ye know him; for he dwelleth with you, and shall be in you.

55

John 15:26 (KJV): ²⁶But when the Comforter is come, whom I will send unto you from the Father, *even* the Spirit of truth, which proceedeth from the Father, he shall testify of me:

John 16:13-14 (KJV): ¹³Howbeit when he, the Spirit of truth, is come, he will guide you into all truth: for he shall not speak of himself; but whatsoever he shall hear, *that* shall he speak: and he will show you things to come. ¹⁴He shall glorify me: for he shall receive of mine, and shall show *it* unto you.

Ephesians 1:13-14 (KJV): ¹³...in whom also after that ye believed, ye were sealed with that holy Spirit of promise, ¹⁴Which is the earnest of our inheritance until the redemption of the purchased possession, unto the praise of his glory.

Jude 1:20 (KJV): [20]But ye, beloved, building up yourselves on your most holy faith, praying in the Holy Ghost,

Romans 8:2 (KJV): [2]For the law of the Spirit of life in Christ Jesus hath made me free from the law of sin and death.

Romans 8:5-6 (KJV): [5]For they that are after the flesh do mind the things of the flesh; but they that are after the Spirit the things of the Spirit. [6]For to be carnally minded *is* death; but to be spiritually minded *is* life and peace.

Romans 8:8-14 (KJV): [8]So then they that are in the flesh cannot please God. [9]But ye are not in the flesh, but in the Spirit, if so be that the Spirit of God dwell in you. Now if any man have not the Spirit of Christ, he is none of his. [10]And if Christ *be* in you, the body is dead because of sin; but the Spirit *is* life because of righteousness. [11]_____, but if the Spirit of him that raised up Jesus from the dead dwell in you, he that raised up Christ from the dead shall also quicken your mortal bodies by his Spirit that dwelleth in you. [12]Therefore, brethren, we are debtors, not to the flesh, to live after the flesh. [13]_____, for if ye live after the flesh, ye shall die: but if ye through the Spirit do mortify the deeds of the body, ye shall live. [14]For as many as are led by the Spirit of God, they are the sons of God.

Romans 8:26-27 (KJV): [26]Likewise the Spirit also helpeth our infirmities: for we know not what we should pray for as we ought: but the Spirit itself maketh intercession for us with groaning which cannot be uttered. [27]And he that searcheth the hearts knoweth what is the mind of the Spirit, because he maketh intercession for the saints according to *the will* of God.

Galatians 3:14 (KJV): ¹⁴That the blessing of Abraham might come on the Gentiles through Jesus Christ; that we might receive the promise of the Spirit through faith.

Galatians 5:16-18 (KJV): ¹⁶*This* I say then, Walk in the Spirit, and ye shall not fulfil the lust of the flesh. ¹⁷For the flesh lusteth against the Spirit, and the Spirit against the flesh: and these are contrary the one to the other: so that ye cannot do the things that ye would. ¹⁸But if ye be led of the Spirit, ye are not under the law.

John 14:26 (KJV): ²⁶But the Comforter, *which is* the Holy Ghost, whom the Father will send in my name, he shall teach you all things, and bring all things to your remembrance, whatsoever I have said unto you.

Plan of Action:

_____, My children are led by the Holy Spirit. But the Holy Spirit will not compete with your flesh. When you choose to die to your flesh and live according to My Word, the Holy Spirit will lead you into all truth and divine knowledge and revelation.

Confession: I am led by the Holy Spirit, not my feelings or my mind. I pull down every natural thought or imagination that exalts itself against the knowledge of God and make it obedient to Christ through my knowledge of the Word of God. No more inspiration but divine revelation!

 JOY/PEACE

_____, there is joy and peace in My promises. The more you trust Me, the more My joy and peace will increase on the inside of you. The unexplainable joy that you experience when in My presence is My secret ingredient for manifesting My strength in your life. My Word is My presence in your life. It is comfort and rest for you. Read it, study it, come to know Me and trust Me, then you will be able to view your life in the light of My Word instead of in the light of the circumstance.

Nehemiah 8:10 (KJV): 10...for *this* day *is* holy unto our Lord: neither be ye sorry; for the joy of the LORD is your strength.

1 Peter 5:7 (KJV): 7Casting all your care upon him; for he careth for you.

John 16:33 (KJV): 33These things I have spoken unto you, that in me ye might have peace. In the world ye shall have tribulation: but be of good cheer; I have overcome the world.

Romans 14:17 (KJV): 17For the kingdom of God is not meat and drink; but righteousness, and peace, and joy in the Holy Ghost.

Philippians 4:4 (KJV): 4Rejoice in the Lord alway: *and* again I say, Rejoice.

Philippians 4:6-7 (KJV): 6_____, be careful for nothing; but in every thing by prayer and supplication with thanksgiving let your requests be made known unto God. 7And the peace of God, which passeth all understanding, shall keep your hearts and minds through Christ Jesus.

Ephesians 2:14 (KJV): ¹⁴For he is our peace, who hath made both one, and hath broken down the middle wall of partition *between us;*

2 Timothy 1:7 (KJV): ⁷_____, for God hath not given us the spirit of fear; but of power, and of love, and of a sound mind.

Matthew 11:28-30 (KJV): ²⁸Come unto me, all ye that labour and are heavy laden, and I will give you rest. ²⁹Take my yoke upon you, and learn of me; for I am meek and lowly in heart: and ye shall find rest unto your souls. ³⁰For my yoke *is* easy, and my burden is light.

James 1:2-3 (KJV): ²My brethren, count it all joy when ye fall into divers temptations; ³Knowing *this,* that the trying of your faith worketh patience.

Isaiah 26:3 (KJV): ³_____, thou wilt keep *him* in perfect peace, *whose* mind is stayed *on thee:* because he trusteth in thee.

Psalms 16:11 (KJV): ¹¹Thou wilt show me the path of life: in thy presence is fulness of joy; at thy right hand *there are* pleasures for evermore.

Psalms 29:11 (KJV): ¹¹The LORD will give strength unto his people; the LORD will bless his people with peace.

Psalms 23:1 (KJV): ¹The LORD *is* my shepherd; I shall not want.

Psalms 30:5 (KJV): ⁵For his anger *endureth but* a moment; in his favour *is* life: weeping may endure for a night, but joy *cometh* in the morning.

59

Psalms 30:11 (KJV): ¹¹Thou hast turned for me my mourning into dancing: thou hast put off my sackcloth, and girded me with gladness;

Psalms 42:5 (KJV): ⁵Why art thou cast down, O my soul? and *why* art thou disquieted in me? hope thou in God: for I shall yet praise him *for* the help of his countenance.

Proverbs 3:1-2 (KJV): ¹My son, forget not my law; but let thine heart keep my commandments: ²For length of days, and long life, and peace, shall they add to thee.

Proverbs 17:22 (KJV): ²²A merry heart doeth good *like* a medicine: but a broken spirit drieth the bones.

60

Plan of Action:

_____, you must choose to allow My joy and peace to overshadow your circumstances. You do this by laughing when the circumstance says you should be crying. I am not moved by circumstances, and neither should you be moved, for your joy and peace are not motivated by the conditions of life, but in the certainty of My Word.

Confession: Circumstances cannot steal my joy and peace, for the joy of the Lord is my strength.

 LOVE BROTHERLY/GOD'S

_____, love is the greatest gift I have given to you. It was love, My love for you, that allowed Me to give My only Son on the cross in exchange for your life. Love is the essence of My Spirit. Everything that I do, have done, and will do is because of the love that I have for you. When you accept Jesus into your life, you will experience the fullness of My love and get infused with My love. I fill you with My ability to love and demonstrate compassion. I desire to express My love through you to a dying world. That is why I have declared to the world that it will know My children by the love that you show. Love is the driving force behind the flow of the supernatural gifts that I have equipped every one of My children with. My love for humanity will flow through you; it is this expression of love that causes healing, miracles, and the supernatural to manifest. _____, don't let your feelings or emotions get in the way of expressing My love. Trust the Holy Spirit, the Comforter, with your emotions, and you will find that My love in you can flow through any situation (John 14:16).

Love-(Brotherly)

John 13:34-35 (KJV): [34]A new commandment I give unto you, That ye love one another; as I have loved you, that ye also love one another. [35]By this shall all *men* know that ye are my disciples, if ye have love one to another.

John 15:12-14 (KJV): [12]This is my commandment, That ye love one another, as I have loved you. [13]Greater love hath no man than *this*, that a man lay down his life for his friends. [14]Ye are my friends, if ye do whatsoever I command you.

1 John 4:18 (KJV): [18]_____, there is no fear in love; but perfect love casteth out fear: because fear hath torment. He that feareth is not made perfect in love.

Galatians 5:6 (KJV): [6]For in Jesus Christ neither circumcision availeth any thing, nor uncircumcision; but faith which worketh by love.

Galatians 5:14 (KJV): [14]For all the law is fulfilled in one word, *even* in this; Thou shalt love thy neighbour as thyself.

1 Corinthians 13:1-8,13 (KJV): [1]Though I speak with the tongues of men and of angels, and have not charity, I am become *as* sounding brass, or a tinkling cymbal. [2]And though I have *the gift of* prophecy, and understand all mysteries, and all knowledge; and though I have all faith, so that I could remove mountains, and have not charity, I am nothing. [3]And though I bestow all my goods to feed *the poor,* and though I give my body to be burned, and have not charity, it profiteth me nothing. [4]Charity suffereth long, *and* is kind; charity envieth not; charity vaunteth not itself, is not puffed up, [5]Doth not behave itself unseemly, seeketh not her own, is not easily provoked, thinketh no evil; [6]Rejoiceth not in iniquity, but rejoiceth in the truth; [7]Beareth all things, believeth all things, hopeth all things, endureth all things. [8]Charity never faileth: but whether *there be* prophecies, they shall fail; whether *there be* tongues, they shall cease; whether *there be* knowledge, it shall vanish away. [13]And now abideth faith, hope, charity, these three; but the greatest of these is charity.

1 John 3:14 (KJV): [14]We know that we have passed from death unto life, because we love the brethren. He that loveth not *his* brother abideth in death.

Romans 13:8-10 (KJV): [8]Owe no man any thing, but to love one another: for he that loveth another hath fulfilled the law. [9]Thou shalt love thy neighbour as thyself. [10]Love worketh no ill to his neighbour: therefore love *is* the fulfilling of the law.

Romans 8:39 (KJV): [39]Nor height, nor depth, nor any other creature, shall be able to separate us from the love of God, which is in Christ Jesus our Lord.

Colossians 3:14 (KJV): [14]And above all these things *put on* charity, which is the bond of perfectness.

Ephesians 5:1-2 (KJV): [1]Be ye therefore followers of God, as dear children; [2]And walk in love, as Christ also hath loved us, and hath given himself for us an offering and a sacrifice to God for a sweetsmelling savour.

63

Love-(God's)

Mark 12:30 (KJV): [30]And thou shalt love the Lord thy God with all thy heart, and with all thy soul, and with all thy mind, and with all thy strength: this is the first commandment.

John 3:16 (KJV): [16]_____, for God so loved the world, that he gave his only begotten Son, that whosoever believeth in him should not perish, but have everlasting life.

John 15:9 (KJV): [9]_____, as the Father hath loved me, so have I loved you: continue ye in my love.

1 John 3:1 (KJV): [1]Behold, what manner of love the Father hath bestowed upon us, that we should be called the sons of God...

Ephesians 2:4-5 (KJV): [4]But God, who is rich in mercy, for his great love wherewith he loved us, [5]Even when we were dead in sins, hath quickened us together with Christ, (by grace ye are saved;)

Proverbs 8:17 (KJV): [17]I love them that love me; and those that seek me early shall find me.

Plan of Action:

_____, choosing to love is an expression of spiritual maturity. I chose to demonstrate My love to a world that rejected me, to the extent that I gave My only Son to die for it, that it might be reconciled to Me. Change your thinking about love. You do not have to feel it in order to give it. Receive My love for you, and I will empower you to love.

Confession: I choose to walk in love toward others every day.

 OBEDIENCE/CHASTENING

_____, obedience/chastening is the *demonstration* of your faith. You cannot have working faith without the corresponding actions of obedience. Your obedience gives power and ability to your faith. However, this is usually the missing link that hinders most believers from possessing My promises. With every promise, there will always be an opportunity for you to exercise your faith through obedience. Your steps of obedience demonstrate your trust in Me and shows Me that I can also trust you with the manifestation of the promise. Obedience to Me is not to take something away from you, but to give something invaluable and life-changing to you.

Many of My children fail to obey Me because they desire to see the "big picture" and know how everything will unfold before they obey. Well, this is not how spiritual matters operate. Spiritual matters operate by faith, not by natural knowledge and understanding. You must obey by faith before you understand the "why."_____, all you need to know is that I am unfolding a plan for your life individually, the entire body of Christ, and the world. If you will heed My Spirit on the inside of you and choose to obey My Word, you will walk in My perfect plan of victory and blessing.

Deuteronomy 6:3 (KJV): [3]Hear therefore, O Israel, and observe to do *it;* that it may be well with thee, and that ye may increase mightily, as the LORD God of thy fathers hath promised thee, in the land that floweth with milk and honey.

Deuteronomy 6:18 (KJV): [18]And thou shalt do *that which is* right and good in the sight of the LORD: that

it may be well with thee, and that thou mayest go in and possess the good land which the LORD sware unto thy fathers,

Deuteronomy 30:15-16 (KJV): 15See, I have set before thee this day life and good, and death and evil; 16In that I command thee this day to love the LORD thy God, to walk in his ways, and to keep his commandments and his statutes and his judgments, that thou mayest live and multiply: and the LORD thy God shall bless thee in the land whither thou goest to possess it.

Deuteronomy 7:12 (KJV): 12Wherefore it shall come to pass, if ye hearken to these judgments, and keep, and do them, that the LORD thy God shall keep unto thee the covenant and the mercy which he sware unto thy fathers:

Deuteronomy 5:29 (KJV): 29O that there were such an heart in them, that they would fear me, and keep all my commandments always, that it might be well with them, and with their children for ever!

Psalms 32:8-10 (KJV): 8I will instruct thee and teach thee in the way which thou shalt go: I will guide thee with mine eye. 9Be ye not as the horse, *or* as the mule, *which* have no understanding: whose mouth must be held in with bit and bridle, lest they come near unto thee. 10 Many sorrows *shall be* to the wicked: but he that trusteth in the LORD, mercy shall compass him about.

Matthew 7:24-25 (KJV): 24_____, therefore whosoever heareth these sayings of mine, and doeth them, I will liken him unto a wise man, which built his house upon a rock: 25And the rain descended, and the floods came, and the winds blew, and beat upon that house; and it fell not: for it was founded upon a rock.

Matthew 5:19 (KJV): [19]Whosoever therefore shall break one of these least commandments, and shall teach men so, he shall be called the least in the kingdom of heaven: but whosoever shall do and teach *them*, the same shall be called great in the kingdom of heaven.

Matthew 7:21 (KJV): [21]Not every one that saith unto me, Lord, Lord, shall enter into the kingdom of heaven; but he that doeth the will of my Father which is in heaven.

John 13:17 (KJV): [17]If ye know these things, happy are ye if ye do them.

John 15:10 (KJV): [10]If ye keep my commandments, ye shall abide in my love; even as I have kept my Father's commandments, and abide in his love.

John 5:24 (KJV): [24]Verily, verily, I say unto you, He that heareth my word, and believeth on him that sent me, hath everlasting life, and shall not come into condemnation; but is passed from death unto life.

John 8:51 (KJV): [51]Verily, verily, I say unto you, If a man keep my saying, he shall never see death.

1 John 2:17 (KJV): [17]And the world passeth away, and the lust thereof: but he that doeth the will of God abideth for ever.

1 John 3:22 (KJV): [22]And whatsoever we ask, we receive of him, because we keep his commandments, and do those things that are pleasing in his sight.

Romans 2:13 (KJV): [13](For not the hearers of the law *are* just before God, but the doers of the law shall be justified.

 Obedience

Galatians 5:16-17 (KJV): [16]*This* I say then, Walk in the Spirit, and ye shall not fulfil the lust of the flesh. [17]For the flesh lusteth against the Spirit, and the Spirit against the flesh: and these are contrary the one to the other: so that ye cannot do the things that ye would.

Plan of Action:

_____, I am calling you to partner with Me and take your position. Respond in obedience to My leading. First, I will lead in subtle ways with simple instructions. This is to help you learn how I speak to your spirit and to give you an opportunity to demonstrate your faith through obedience. As you faithfully obey, I will lead you into the deeper things of My Spirit, and your "purpose-picture" will become clearer and clearer. _____, I not only reveal Myself to those that trust Me but, even the more, to those that I can trust to obey Me.

Confession: Father, I desire to partner with You to accomplish Your plan on the earth. I have determined in my heart to obey Your Word and Your spiritual leading.

68

 PRAYER

_____, prayer is essential to our fellowship. Simply defined, prayer is communication with Me. You cannot fight against spiritual strongholds and powers of darkness with natural weapons; you fight with spiritual weapons and prayer is your most powerful device. **Prayer** is **p**ower **r**eleased **at** **y**our **e**arnest **r**equest. Prayer is My agent for change! In praying, you are asking Me and giving Me permission to operate on devil-claimed territory, for Satan is the god of this world. Prayer keeps him from being the god of *your* world. I will not violate My Word or your will; therefore, I need your permission and cooperation to work in your life. _____, prayer is making your request known unto Me and being assured of the results. It is not begging. You beg from one who is withholding something from you. _____, I am not withholding. You are My child, and it is My desire and delight to answer you and grant your petition. You only need to ask and then continue to thank Me by faith for the results.

Mark 11:23-24 (KJV): ²³For verily I say unto you, That whosoever shall say unto this mountain, Be thou removed, and be thou cast into the sea; and shall not doubt in his heart, but shall believe that those things which he saith shall come to pass; he shall have whatsoever he saith. ²⁴ Therefore I say unto you, _____, what things soever ye desire, when ye pray, believe that ye receive *them*, and ye shall have *them*.

Matthew 21:22 (KJV): ²²And all things, whatsoever ye shall ask in prayer, believing, ye shall receive.

Matthew 7:7-11 (KJV): 7_____,
ask, and it shall be given you; seek, and ye shall find;
knock, and it shall be opened unto you: 8For every one
that asketh receiveth; and he that seeketh findeth; and to
him that knocketh it shall be opened. 9Or what man is
there of you, whom if his son ask bread, will he give him a
stone? 10Or if he ask a fish, will he give him a serpent? 11If
ye then, being evil, know how to give good gifts unto your
children, how much more shall your Father which is in
heaven give good things to them that ask him?

Matthew 6:6-8 (KJV): 6But thou, when thou prayest,
enter into thy closet, and when thou hast shut thy door,
pray to thy Father which is in secret; and thy Father which
seeth in secret shall reward thee openly. 7But when ye
pray, use not vain repetitions, as the heathen *do:* for they
think that they shall be heard for their much speaking. 8Be
not ye therefore like unto them: for your Father knoweth
what things ye have need of, before ye ask him.

Matthew 18:18-19 (KJV): 18Verily I say unto you,
_____, whatsoever ye shall bind on
earth shall be bound in heaven: and whatsoever ye shall
loose on earth shall be loosed in heaven. 19Again I say unto
you, That if two of you shall agree on earth as touching
any thing that they shall ask, it shall be done for them of
my Father which is in heaven.

John 15:16 (KJV): 16_____, ye have
not chosen me, but I have chosen you, and ordained you,
that ye should go and bring forth fruit, and *that* your fruit
should remain: that whatsoever ye shall ask of the Father
in my name, he may give it you.

John 14:13-14 (KJV): 13And whatsoever ye shall ask in
my name, that will I do, that the Father may be glorified
in the Son. 14_____, if ye shall ask any
thing in my name, I will do *it.*

John 16:23-24 (KJV): [23]And in that day ye shall ask me nothing. Verily, verily, I say unto you, Whatsoever ye shall ask the Father in my name, he will give *it* you. [24]Hitherto have ye asked nothing in my name: ask, and ye shall receive, that your joy may be full.

John 15:7 (KJV): [7]If ye abide in me, and my words abide in you, ye shall ask what ye will, and it shall be done unto you.

1 John 3:22 (KJV): [22]And whatsoever we ask, we receive of him, because we keep his commandments, and do those things that are pleasing in his sight.

1 John 5:14-15 (KJV): [14]And this is the confidence that we have in him, that, if we ask any thing according to his will, he heareth us: [15]And if we know that he hear us, whatsoever we ask, we know that we have the petitions that we desired of him.

James 5:16 (KJV): [16]Confess *your* faults one to another, and pray one for another, that ye may be healed. The effectual fervent prayer of a righteous man availeth much.

Philippians 4:6-7 (KJV): [6]_____, be careful for nothing; but in every thing by prayer and supplication with thanksgiving let your requests be made known unto God. 7And the peace of God, which passeth all understanding, shall keep your hearts and minds through Christ Jesus.

1 Thessalonians 5:17 (KJV):
[17]_____, pray without ceasing.

Romans 8:26-27 (KJV): [26]Likewise the Spirit also helpeth our infirmities: for we know not what we should pray for as we ought: but the Spirit itself maketh

Prayer

intercession for us with groanings which cannot be uttered. [27]And he that searcheth the hearts knoweth what is the mind of the Spirit, because he maketh intercession for the saints according to *the will of* God.

1 Corinthians 14:2 (KJV): [2]For he that speaketh in an *unknown* tongue speaketh not unto men, but unto God: for no man understandeth *him;* howbeit in the spirit he speaketh mysteries.

1 Corinthians 14:14 (KJV): [14]For if I pray in an *unknown* tongue, my spirit prayeth, but my understanding is unfruitful.

1 Timothy 2:1 (KJV): [1]I exhort therefore, that, first of all, supplications, prayers, intercessions, *and* giving of thanks, be made for all men;

Ephesians 6:18 (KJV): [18]Praying always with all prayer and supplication in the Spirit, and watching thereunto with all perseverance and supplication for all saints;

1 Peter 5:7 (KJV): [7]Casting all your care upon him; for he careth **for you.**

Jeremiah 33:3 (KJV): [3]_____, call unto me, and I will answer thee, and show thee great and mighty things, which thou knowest not.

Jeremiah 29:12 (KJV): [12]Then shall ye call upon me, and ye shall go and pray unto me, and I will hearken unto you.

Isaiah 65:24 (KJV): [24]And it shall come to pass, that before they call, I will answer; and while they are yet speaking, I will hear.

Psalms 50:15 (KJV): [15]And call upon me in the day of trouble: I will deliver thee, and thou shalt glorify me.

Psalms 145:18-19 (KJV): [18] The LORD is nigh unto all them that call upon him, to all that call upon him in truth. [19] He will fulfil the desire of them that fear him: he also will hear their cry, and will save them.

Plan of Action:

_____, pray, pray, pray. Pray without ceasing or have a continual spirit of prayer. Set aside time to spend with Me before you start your day. Make this time a priority for your life and stay committed. _____, remember, prayer is your spiritual lifeline. It keeps the cares of the world from overtaking you and stealing your joy. Keep prayer as a daily priority and cast every weight of concern on Me then rest in the peaceful assurance of My provision and blessing for you. Then your peace and endued power will effectively impact the lives of those around you.

Confession: I make prayer a daily priority for my life. I change my worries into prayers. When I pray, in faith, I believe that I receive.

PROSPERITY

_____, prosperity in every area of your life is My desire for you. My prosperity is not limited to material things. My children should prosper in spirit, soul, relationships, health, and wealth. Prosperity is possessing in abundance that which you need with some remaining to share with others. Look at the life of Jesus. Jesus understood that He had access to the endless supply of My kingdom to meet His every need; therefore, Jesus was always giving. When the disciples became concerned about how they would pay the taxes or feed the multitude, Jesus just simply depended upon Me and every need was supernaturally met. Jesus never gave thought to lack or not enough. Jesus lived upon the earth the way Adam lived during his short stay in the Garden of Eden-totally dependent upon Me to meet His need. Jesus possessed, _in Him,_ enough for Himself and others. That is why those that believe that He was poor have misunderstood and misinterpreted the Scriptures. To be poor is to have a lack of supply or to possess less than what is necessary to meet your own need, never to mention the need of others. I never command anyone to hoard, withhold, or heap up for oneself. I only command you to GIVE. My Word has actually said that it is more blessed to give than to receive. Well, it would be quite unfair for Me to ask My "poor" children to give. Therefore, in My mind, My children are not poor, only prosperous. Many have no problem believing that I desire spiritual prosperity, but most struggle with the belief that I equally desire to bless My children financially. Well, no good father wants his children to barely make it or to be poor. A good father wants the absolute best for his children. _____, I am greater than a natural father. I, your **heavenly Father,** desire to bless you over and above all that

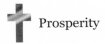
you could ask or think. My children are blessed to be a blessing to others and to establish My kingdom on the earth. Yes, many that are ungodly do prosper, but they must toil for their prosperity. My blessings make you rich and add no sorrow, for My prosperity also yields in you that which is eternal. Your relationships will not have to pay the price for your prosperity. Nothing will go lacking. When your faith is coupled just right with your character and obedience, then the window of heaven is opened up to you. I will bless you and enable YOU to prosper in whatever you put your hands to. I connect with you and put My *super* on your *natural*. Then your victories are effortless. A little will yield much; small beginnings will have great endings. You will *know* when My window of blessing has been opened up to you! And like Jesus, you will live on the earth just as Adam lived in the garden-totally dependent upon Me-and I never fail.

Matthew 6:33 (KJV): 33But seek ye first the kingdom of God, and his righteousness; and all these things shall be added unto you.

3 John 1:2 (KJV): 2Beloved, I wish above all things that thou mayest prosper and be in health, even as thy soul prospereth.

John 10:10 (KJV): 10The thief cometh not, but for to steal, and to kill, and to destroy: I am come that they might have life, and that they might have *it* more abundantly.

Deuteronomy 8:18 (KJV): 18But thou shalt remember the LORD thy God: for *it is* he that giveth thee power to get wealth, that he may establish his covenant which he sware unto thy fathers, as *it is* this day.

2 Corinthians 8:9 (KJV): 9_____,
for ye know the grace of our Lord Jesus Christ, that,
though he was rich, yet for your sakes he became poor,
that ye through his poverty might be rich.

Mark 10:28-30 (KJV): 28Then Peter began to say unto
him, Lo, we have left all, and have followed thee. 29And
Jesus answered and said, Verily I say unto you, There is no
man that hath left house, or brethren, or sisters, or father,
or mother, or wife, or children, or lands, for my sake, and
the gospel's, 30But he shall receive an hundredfold now in
this time, houses, and brethren, and sisters, and mothers,
and children, and lands, with persecutions; and in the
world to come eternal life.

Philippians 4:19 (KJV): 19But my God shall supply
all your need according to his riches in glory by Christ
Jesus.

2 Corinthians 9:6-11 (KJV): 6But this I *say,* He which
soweth sparingly shall reap also sparingly; and he which
soweth bountifully shall reap also bountifully. 7Every
man according as he purposeth in his heart, *so let him
give;* not grudgingly, or of necessity: for God loveth
a cheerful giver. 8And God is able to make all grace
abound toward you; that ye, always having all sufficiency
in all *things,* may abound to every good work: 9(As it is
written, He hath dispersed abroad; he hath given to the
poor: his righteousness remaineth for ever. 10Now he that
ministereth seed to the sower both minister bread for *your*
food, and multiply your seed sown, and increase the fruits
of your righteousness;) 11Being enriched in every thing to
all bountifulness, which causeth through us thanksgiving
to God.

Luke 6:38 (KJV): 38_____, give,
and it shall be given unto you; good measure, pressed

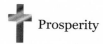

down, and shaken together, and running over, shall men give into your bosom. For with the same measure that ye mete withal it shall be measured to you again.

1 Timothy 6:6 (KJV): ⁶But godliness with contentment is great gain.

1 Timothy 6:17-19 (KJV): ¹⁷Charge them that are rich in this world, that they be not highminded, nor trust in uncertain riches, but in the living God, who giveth us richly all things to enjoy; ¹⁸That they do good, that they be rich in good works, ready to distribute, willing to communicate; ¹⁹Laying up in store for themselves a good foundation against the time to come, that they may lay hold on eternal life.

Matthew 6:19-21 (KJV): ¹⁹Lay not up for yourselves treasures upon earth, where moth and rust doth corrupt, and where thieves break through and steal: ²⁰But lay up for yourselves treasures in heaven, where neither moth nor rust doth corrupt, and where thieves do not break through nor steal: ²¹For where your treasure is, there will your heart be also.

Psalms 34:9-10 (KJV): ⁹O fear the LORD, ye his saints: for *there is* no want to them that fear him. 10   The young lions do lack, and suffer hunger: but they that seek the LORD shall not want any good *thing*.

Isaiah 1:19 (KJV): ¹⁹If ye be willing and obedient, ye shall eat the good of the land:

Deuteronomy 29:9 (KJV): ⁹Keep therefore the words of this covenant, and do them, that ye may prosper in all that ye do.

Deuteronomy 28:1-2 (KJV): ¹And it shall come to pass, if thou shalt hearken diligently unto the voice of the

LORD thy God, to observe *and* to do all his commandments which I command thee this day, that the LORD thy God will set thee on high above all nations of the earth: ²And all these blessings shall come on thee, and overtake thee, if thou shalt hearken unto the voice of the LORD thy God.

Joshua 1:8 (KJV): ⁸This book of the law shall not depart out of thy mouth; but thou shalt meditate therein day and night, that thou mayest observe to do according to all that is written therein: for then thou shalt make thy way prosperous, and then thou shalt have good success.

Job 36:11 (KJV): ¹¹If they obey and serve *him,* they shall spend their days in prosperity, and their years in pleasures.

Psalms 1:3 (KJV): ³And he shall be like a tree planted by the rivers of water, that bringeth forth his fruit in his season; his leaf also shall not wither; and whatsoever he doeth shall prosper.

Malachi 3:10-12 (KJV): ¹⁰Bring ye all the tithes into the storehouse, that there may be meat in mine house, and prove me now herewith, saith the LORD of hosts, if I will not open you the windows of heaven, and pour you out a blessing, *that there shall* not *be room* enough *to receive it.* ¹¹And I will rebuke the devourer for your sakes, and he shall not destroy the fruits of your ground; neither shall your vine cast her fruit before the time in the field, saith the LORD of hosts. ¹²And all nations shall call you blessed: for ye shall be a delightsome land, saith the LORD of hosts.

Plan of Action:

_____, I have given you a sure way to prosper. It is being obedient to My Word concerning tithing and giving. If you will put My kingdom first and trust Me with the tenth of your increase, I have promised to bless you with a blessing you cannot contain. You must also be obedient to give and sow seed. Seed sown on good ground always yields a return. As you walk by faith and not by sight, I will lead you into prosperity in every area of your life.

Confession: I am redeemed from poverty and lack. Jesus is my Shepherd; I shall not want for anything.

 SALVATION

_____, Adam's sin caused every human to be born with a sinful nature. This is the same nature that resides within Satan, and he knew just what would happen to Adam when he disobeyed Me. Satan knew that Adam, just like Satan, would be evicted from his dwelling place, dismissed from My presence, and that our fellowship would be severed. But what Satan did not know was that Adam was still Mine. I created him and breathed My life into him. Therefore, I sent Jesus, My Son, to undo the sin of Adam and build the bridge of reconciliation to humanity, that My children will have unhindered and unlimited access to Me and My kingdom. _____, Jesus came to the earth not from man's seed, but from My seed. He offered Himself as a sinless sacrifice. He had to die a physical and a spiritual death in order to satisfy the requirement for the penalty of sin. Jesus accomplished the perfect plan of redemption (Rom. 5:12-20)! He paid the full price for the remission of sin and the letter of the Law. There is not one cent left to be paid! Therefore, Jesus is the ONLY One that can save you from the penalty of the sin nature that Adam passed on to all of humanity. Believing on Jesus is the ONLY key that gives you access into My kingdom and My presences. It is confessing and believing in His finished work at Calvary that causes you to become righteous, for at the moment that you believe on Jesus, you die a spiritual death just as Jesus did and you are spiritually raised to a new, everlasting life just as Jesus was. Now you must study and meditate on My Word. Then continually rehearse and speak forth your salvation in order to partake of and experience the fullness of its benefits here on the earth.

Romans 10:9-10 (KJV): ⁹That if thou shalt confess with thy mouth the Lord Jesus, and shalt believe in thine heart that God hath raised him from the dead, thou shalt be saved. ¹⁰For with the heart man believeth unto righteousness; and with the mouth confession is made unto salvation.

1 Timothy 2:5-6 (KJV): ⁵For *there* is one God, and one mediator between God and men, the man Christ Jesus; 6Who gave himself a ransom for all, to be testified in due time.

John 3:16-17 (KJV): ¹⁶ _____, for God so loved the world, that he gave his only begotten Son, that whosoever believeth in him should not perish, but have everlasting life. ¹⁷For God sent not his Son into the world to condemn the world; but that the world through him might be saved.

John 14:6 (KJV): ⁶Jesus saith unto him, I am the way, the truth, and the life: no man cometh unto the Father, but by me.

John 10:1 (KJV): ¹Verily, verily, I say unto you, He that entereth not by the door into the sheepfold, but climbeth up some other way, the same is a thief and a robber.

John 10:9 (KJV): ⁹I am the door: by me if any man enter in, he shall be saved, and shall go in and out, and find pasture.

John 10:17 (KJV): ¹⁷Therefore doth my Father love me, because I lay down my life, that I might take it again.

John 10:27-28 (KJV): ²⁷My sheep hear my voice, and I know them, and they follow me: ²⁸And I give unto them eternal life; and they shall never perish, neither shall any *man* pluck them out of my hand.

John 6:47 (KJV): [47]Verily, verily, I say unto you, He that believeth on me hath everlasting life.

John 1:12-13 (KJV): [12]But as many as received him, to them gave he power to become the sons of God, *even* to them that believe on his name: [13]Which were born, not of blood, nor of the will of the flesh, nor of the will of man, but of God.

John 11:25-26 (KJV): [25]Jesus said unto her, I am the resurrection, and the life: he that believeth in me, though he were dead, yet shall he live: [26]And whosoever liveth and believeth in me shall never die. Believest thou this?

Mark 8:38 (KJV): [38]Whosoever therefore shall be ashamed of me and of my words in this adulterous and sinful generation; of him also shall the Son of man be ashamed, when he cometh in the glory of his Father with the holy angels.

2 Corinthians 5:17 (KJV): [17]Therefore if any man *be* in Christ, *he* is a new creature: old things are passed away; behold, all things are become new.

2 Corinthians 5:21 (KJV): [21]For he hath made him *to be* sin for us, who knew no sin; that we might be made the righteousness of God in him.

2 Corinthians 7:10 (KJV): [10]For godly sorrow worketh repentance to salvation not to be repented of: but the sorrow of the world worketh death.

Romans 5:8 (KJV): [8]But God commendeth his love toward us, in that, while we were yet sinners, Christ died for us.

Galatians 3:13 (KJV): ¹³_____,
Christ hath redeemed us from the curse of the law, being
made a curse for us: for it is written, Cursed *is* every one
that hangeth on a tree:

Galatians 3:21-27 (KJV): ²¹*Is* the law then against the
promises of God? God forbid: for if there had been a law
given which could have given life, verily righteousness
should have been by the law. ²²But the scripture hath
concluded all under sin, that the promise by faith of Jesus
Christ might be given to them that believe. ²³But before
faith came, we were kept under the law, shut up unto the
faith which should afterwards be revealed. ²⁴Wherefore
the law was our schoolmaster *to bring us* unto Christ,
that we might be justified by faith. ²⁵But after that faith
is come, we are no longer under a schoolmaster. ²⁶For ye
are all the children of God by faith in Christ Jesus. ²⁷For
as many of you as have been baptized into Christ have put
on Christ.

Galatians 4:3-7 (KJV): ³Even so we, when we were
children, were in bondage under the elements of the
world: 4But when the fullness of the time was come,
God sent forth his Son, made of a woman, made under
the law, 5To redeem them that were under the law, that
we might receive the adoption of sons. 6And because ye
are sons, God hath sent forth the Spirit of his Son into
your hearts, crying, Abba, Father. 7Wherefore thou art no
more a servant, but a son; and if a son, then an heir of God
through Christ.

Ephesians 1:13 (KJV): ¹³In whom ye also *trusted*,
after that ye heard the word of truth, the gospel of your
salvation: in whom also after that ye believed, ye were
sealed with that holy Spirit of promise,

83

Colossians 1:12-14 (KJV): ¹²Giving thanks unto the Father, which hath made us meet to be partakers of the inheritance of the saints in light: ¹³Who hath delivered us from the power of darkness, and hath translated us into the kingdom of his dear Son: ¹⁴In whom we have redemption through his blood, *even* the forgiveness of sins:

Titus 3:4-7 (KJV): ⁴But after that the kindness and love of God our Saviour toward man appeared, ⁵Not by works of righteousness which we have done, but according to his mercy he saved us, by the washing of regeneration, and renewing of the Holy Ghost; ⁶Which he shed on us abundantly through Jesus Christ our Saviour; ⁷That being justified by his grace, we should be made heirs according to the hope of eternal life.

84

1 John 5:11-12 (KJV): ¹¹And this is the record, that God hath given to us eternal life, and this life is in his Son. ¹²_____, he that hath the Son hath life; *and* he that hath not the Son of God hath not life.

John 3:3-7 (KJV): ³Jesus answered and said unto him, Verily, verily, I say unto thee, Except a man be born again, he cannot see the kingdom of God. ⁴Nicodemus saith unto him, How can a man be born when he is old? Can he enter the second time into his mother's womb, and be born? ⁵Jesus answered, Verily, verily, I say unto thee, Except a man be born of water and *of* the Spirit, he cannot enter into the kingdom of God. ⁶That which is born of the flesh is flesh; and that which is born of the Spirit is spirit. ⁷Marvel not that I said unto thee, Ye must be born again.

1 John 2:1-2 (KJV): ¹My little children, these things write I unto you, that ye sin not. And if any man sin, we have an advocate with the Father, Jesus Christ the righteous: ²And he is the propitiation for our sins: and not for ours only, but also for *the sins of* the whole world.

Revelation 3:20 (KJV): [20]Behold, I stand at the door, and knock: if any man hear my voice, and open the door, I will come in to him, and will sup with him, and he with me.

Plan of Action:

_____, settle in your belief that Jesus is the only way to be redeemed from the sinful nature of man and the penalty of sin. Accept Jesus into your heart by believing and confessing out of your mouth His completed work at Calvary. Jesus' death did more than take away your sin; it released you from the grip and control of Satan and freed you to an entirely new life unto Me for My glory. So study My Word daily to grow in the knowledge of your redemption. The more you know about your redemption and the inheritance that I have provided for you, the more authority you will exercise on the earth and the more victory you will experience.

Confession: I accept Jesus as the ONLY way, the truth, and the life. I am the righteousness of God in Christ Jesus.

 WORSHIP

_____, worship ties the knot in our relationship. Those that worship Me are so convinced of My love for them that giving their entire lives to Me is not a burden, but a desire. Worship is your complete and total devotion to, honor of, and reverence of a person, place, or thing. True worship is a lifestyle, and you were created to worship Me and Me alone. I do not demand your worship as would a tyrant or a master, but as a loving Father, I longingly desire your worship. I do not desire your worship to control you, but that you will trust Me to lead you into your promised land, into the place that I have for you flowing with milk and honey, flowing with the blessings that I have just for you. _____, you do not get into this place of blessing by standing at a distance. You get into this place by drawing close to Me, by developing an intimate relationship with Me, and becoming hungry and thirsty for Me. So _____, I bid you come closer to Me with a heart of worship.

John 4:23-24 (KJV): 23But the hour cometh, and now is, when the true worshippers shall worship the Father in spirit and in truth: for the Father seeketh such to worship him. 24God *is* a Spirit: and they that worship him must worship *him* in spirit and in truth.

Philippians 3:3 (KJV): 3_____, for we are the circumcision, which worship God in the spirit, and rejoice in Christ Jesus, and have no confidence in the flesh.

86

Matthew 4:10 (KJV): ¹⁰Then saith Jesus unto him, Get thee hence, Satan: for it is written, Thou shalt worship the Lord thy God, and him only shalt thou serve.

Isaiah 6:3 (KJV): ³And one cried unto another, and said, Holy, holy, holy, *is* the LORD of hosts: the whole earth *is* full of his glory.

Psalms 95:6 (KJV): ⁶O come, let us worship and bow down: let us kneel before the LORD our maker.

Psalms 150:1-6 (KJV): ¹Praise ye the LORD. Praise God in his sanctuary: praise him in the firmament of his power. ²Praise him for his mighty acts: praise him according to his excellent greatness. ³Praise him with the sound of the trumpet: praise him with the psaltery and harp. ⁴Praise him with the timbrel and dance: praise him with stringed instruments and organs. ⁵ Praise him upon the loud cymbals: praise him upon the high sounding cymbals. ⁶ Let every thing that hath breath praise the LORD. Praise ye the LORD.

Revelation 4:11 (KJV): ¹¹Thou art worthy, O Lord, to receive glory and honour and power: for thou hast created all things, and for thy pleasure they are and were created.

Psalms 30:12 (KJV): ¹²To the end that *my* glory may sing praise to thee, and not be silent. O LORD my God, I will give thanks unto thee for ever.

Psalms 92:1-2 (KJV): ¹ *It is* a good *thing* to give thanks unto the LORD, and to sing praises unto thy name, O most High: ² To show forth thy lovingkindness in the morning, and thy faithfulness every night,...

Worship

Plan of Action:

_____, let your lifestyle be
your ultimate act of worship of Me, not just the
lifting of your hands in the sanctuary. Allow Me
and Me alone to sit on the throne of your heart.

Confession: I was created to worship the Lord
my God. My heavenly Father sits on the throne
of my heart. Everything in me will worship Him.

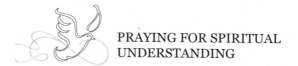 PRAYING FOR SPIRITUAL
UNDERSTANDING

Ephesians 1:17-23 (KJV): ¹⁷That the God of our Lord Jesus Christ, the Father of glory, may give unto *me* the spirit of wisdom and revelation in the knowledge of him: ¹⁸The eyes of *my* understanding being enlightened; that *I* may know what is the hope of his calling, and what the riches of the glory of his inheritance in the saints, ¹⁹And what is the exceeding greatness of his power *towards me* who believe, according to the working of his mighty power, ²⁰Which he wrought in Christ, when he raised him from the dead, and set him at his own right hand in the heavenly places, ²¹Far above all principality, and power, and might, and dominion, and every name that is named, not only in this world, but also in that which is to come: ²²And hath put all things under his feet, and gave him to be the head over all things to the church, ²³Which is his body, the fulness of him that filleth all in all.

Ephesians 3:14-21 (KJV): ¹⁴For this cause I bow my knees unto the Father of our Lord Jesus Christ, ¹⁵Of whom the whole family in heaven and earth is named, ¹⁶That he would grant *me,* according to the riches of his glory, to be strengthened with might by his Spirit in the inner man; ¹⁷That Christ may dwell in *my* heart by faith; that *I,* being rooted and grounded in love, 18May be able to comprehend with all saints what is the breadth, and length, and depth, and height; ¹⁹And to know the love of Christ, which passeth knowledge, that *I* might be filled with all the fulness of God. ²⁰Now unto him that is able to do exceeding abundantly above all that I ask or think, according to the power that worketh in me, ²¹Unto him be glory in the church by Christ Jesus throughout all ages, world without end. Amen.

All promise Scriptures have remained in their original form throughout this book; only your name has been inserted at an appropriate place. The prayers for spiritual understanding have been modified to make them read in first person.

Note:

This promise book is not intended to, nor could it ever, replace the studying of your Bible. The time you spend with the Father in prayer, fasting, and studying His Word will enhance the opportunity for these Scriptures to grow and take root in your heart. This book only highlights a few subjects that will help you begin to lay a foundation for a strong and intimate relationship with your heavenly Father.

 HOW TO ORDER YOUR COPY

www.heavenlypromisestome.org

or

PO box 1082, Waxhaw, NC 28173

or

(704) 597-8008

ABOUT THE AUTHORS

Motivated and active servants of God, Dwain and Anita Byrum have dedicated their lives to learning and spreading the Gospel of Jesus Christ. As Bible class instructors, they're firmly committed to teaching God's Word. In addition to their years of developing, executing and contributing to the Body of Christ, they've provided spiritual based counseling to engaged couples, at premarital preparation programs. Dwain, an entrepreneur and Anita, a healthcare professional, both greatly inspire people through encouraging FAITH elevation and relationship building with God. As devoted members of Grace Christian Center in Charlotte, NC, they support the mission of the ministry efforts to restore and empower lives daily.

Living in Waxhaw, NC, Dwain and Anita are proud parents of one son and three daughters.

 JOURNAL

108